Serving Children with Disabilities

LAUDAN Y. ARON
PAMELA J. LOPREST
C. EUGENE STEUERLE

Serving Children with Disabilities

A Systematic Look at the Programs

THE URBAN INSTITUTE PRESS
Washington, D.C.

Library of Congress Cataloging in Publication Data

Serving Children with Disabilities: A Systematic Look
at the Programs / Laudan Y. Aron, Pamela J. Loprest, and
C. Eugene Steuerle

1. Handicapped children—Government policy—United States.
2. Handicapped children—Services for—United States.
I. Loprest, Pamela. II. Steuerle, C. Eugene, 1946–   . III. Title.

| HV888.5.A76 | 1996 | 95-45762 |
| 362.4'083—dc20 | | CIP |

ISBN 0-87766-651-2 (paper, alk. paper)
ISBN 0-87766-650-4 (cloth, alk. paper)

Printed in the United States of America.

Distributed in North America by:
University Press of America
4720 Boston Way
Lanham, MD 20706

THE URBAN INSTITUTE is a nonprofit policy research and educational organization established in Washington, D.C., in 1968. Its staff investigates the social and economic problems confronting the nation and public and private means to alleviate them. The Institute disseminates significant findings of its research through the publications program of its Press. The goals of the Institute are to sharpen thinking about societal problems and efforts to solve them, improve government decisions and performance, and increase citizen awareness of important policy choices.

Through work that ranges from broad conceptual studies to administrative and technical assistance, Institute researchers contribute to the stock of knowledge available to guide decision making in the public interest.

Conclusions or opinions expressed in Institute publications are those of the authors and do not necessarily reflect the views of staff members, officers or trustees of the Institute, advisory groups, or any organizations that provide financial support to the Institute.

LIST OF ACRONYMS

ACF	Administration on Children and Families
ADA	Americans with Disabilities Act
ADD	Administration on Developmental Disabilities
ADL	Activities of Daily Living
AFDC	Aid to Families with Dependent Children
ALJ	Administrative Law Judge
BD	Behavior Disordered
BEH	Behaviorally-Emotionally Handicapped
CASSP	Child and Adolescent Service System Program
CMHS	Center for Mental Health Services
CPS	Current Population Survey
CPSP	Carolina Policy Studies Program
CSHCN	Children with Special Health Care Needs
DBRA	Disability Benefits Reform Act
DD	Developmental Disability
DDS	Disability Determination Services
DI	Disability Insurance
ESEA	Elementary and Secondary Education Act
EPSDT	Early and Periodic Screening, Diagnosis and Treatment
FMAP	Federal Medical Assistant Percentage
GAO	General Accounting Office
HCBS	Home and Community-Based Services
HCFA	Health Care Financing Administration
HHS	Health and Human Services
IADL	Instrumental Activity of Daily Living
ICF	Intermediate Care Facilities
ICIDH	International Classification of Impairments, Disabilities, and Handicaps
IDEA	Individuals with Disabilities Education Act
IEP	Individualized Education Plan
IFA	Individual Functional Assessment

IFSP	Individual Family Service Plan
MCH	Maternal and Child Health
MR	Mental Retardation
NEC*TAS	National Early Childhood Technical Assistance System
NF	Nursing Facilities
NHIS	National Health Interview Survey
NIMH	National Institute of Mental Health
NMCUES	National Medical Care Utilization and Expenditure Survey
OASI	Old Age Survivors Insurance
OSEP	Office of Special Education Programs
OSERS	Office of Special Education and Rehabilitative Services
PADD	Protection and Advocacy Program for People with Developmental Disabilities
PAMII	Protection and Advocacy Program for Mentally Ill Individuals
SCH	Services for Children with Handicaps
SEAs	State Educational Agencies
SED	Severely Emotionally Disturbed
SIDS	Sudden Infant Death Syndrome
SIPP	Survey of Income and Program Participation
SMHA	State Mental Health Agencies
SOP	State Operated Programs
SSA	Social Security Administration
SSBG	Social Services Block Grant
SSDI	Social Security Disability Insurance
SSI	Supplemental Security Income
TEFRA	Tax Equity and Fiscal Responsibility Act
VR	Vocational Rehabilitation

ACKNOWLEDGMENTS

This study was originally conceived of by Steven Sandell, now with the Social Security Administration. He was particularly concerned with the lack of a broader base of information from which policymakers, who were making decisions on programs affecting these children, could proceed. Shortly after this study was underway, the National Commission on Childhood Disability was established to review the assistance given to children with disabilities under the Supplemental Security Income (SSI) program. Earlier versions of this study were submitted in writing and in testimony before this commission. The commission was in the process of releasing its findings and recommendations as this book went to press.

Three individuals, in addition to the authors, contributed directly to the writing of this report. Ronald Conley of Pelavin Research Institute helped draft several sections, participated in numerous conversations and reviews of the study, and shared with us his insights from years of experience in this area. Gordon Mermin of the Urban Institute contributed the appendix on International Perspectives on Children with Disabilities and provided excellent research assistance throughout the course of this study. Rune Simeonsson of the University of North Carolina at Chapel Hill contributed drafts on diagnostic, classification, and measurement issues and was invaluable in helping us better understand the perspectives of the special education community.

This study was funded in part by the U.S. Department of Health and Human Services and benefited greatly from the input of many in government, universities, research institutes, national associations, private groups, and foundations. Through meetings and phone conversations (perhaps more than some of them care to remember), these individuals provided us with critical program information, assisted us in interpreting it, referred us to other important individuals and organizations, reviewed sections of our report, and shared with us their wisdom and support. Space limitations do not allow us to list each person's contribution, but, in alphabetical order, we thank the following:

Michele Adler	Glenn Fujiura	Deborah Perry
Barbara Aliza	Constance Garner	Virginia Reno
Cynthia Bascetta	Robert Gettings	Jane Ross
Anne Benson	Susan Goodman	Kalman Rupp
David Braddock	Ellen Habenicht	Jack Schmulowitz
Valerie Bradley	Vera Hollen	Rhoda Schulzinger
Marsha Brauen	Henry Ireys	Charles Scott
Scott Brown	Arthur Kahn	Diane Sondheimer
Martha Burt	Donald Kates	Sean Sweeney
Brian Burwell	K. Charlie Lakin	Nancy Treusch
Tom Coakley	David Liska	Craig Turner
Louis Danielson	Margaret McGlaughlin	Ilene Zeitzer
Marilyn Ellwood	Karen Obermaier	
Alison Evans	Thomas Parrish	

In addition, several individuals deserve special mention for having reviewed much or all of this study and provided valuable comments that have greatly improved this book: Jerry Mashaw of Yale Law School, Paul Newacheck of the University of California, San Francisco, James Perrin of Harvard Medical School, and John Reiss of the Institute for Child Health Policy. Ann Guillot and Sheila Lopez assisted with the day-to-day management and organization of the project.

CONTENTS

Figures

FOREWORD

In the world of scarce resources within which policy decisions have to be made, difficult tradeoffs are inevitable. Value judgments are an inevitable part of making these tradeoffs—society's assessment of the relative values of benefits and costs to one group versus another. Such normative judgments are always hard, but they are impossible to make in an informed way without a systematic framework for assessing the tradeoffs being made. Comparisons across program areas are the most intractable, because there is no consensus on a common metric to measure, for example, the benefits of health care versus, say, income security. Even within program areas, the policy-making process often has little systematic information to work with. Public programs for children with disabilities is a good case in point.

The authors of *Serving Children with Disabilities* begin the task of bringing systematic thinking to bear on this large and diverse set of public programs. As they set on their task they discovered that there was not even a simple accounting of the combined expenditures made by government programs for children with disabilities, much less any consistency in identifying and measuring their needs.

This book provides the first comprehensive accounting of public expenditures on children with disabilities. It also presents the first detailed comparison across all the major programs by level of jurisdiction, benefit type and generosity, eligibility conditions, and disability definitions.

But the book does much more than this. It presents a set of guiding principles for thinking about how best to allocate new resources or reallocate the resources already being spent on these children and their families. Although principles cannot set society's priorities, the potential gains from a systematic approach are enormous. A society that forces itself to be explicit in the choices it makes is likely to use its resources much more effectively in meeting social needs than if it abandons the effort in favor of piecemeal action in response to political pressures.

As we approach the 21st century, this country is engaged in some much needed rethinking about social program directions, including a search for ways to simplify programs, integrate efforts, and identify more cost-effective ways to respond to public needs. I hope that the systematic framework presented here will help in the rethinking effort.

William Gorham
President

Part One

OVERVIEW AND PRINCIPLES

Chapter One

INTRODUCTION

Few individuals arouse such deep and passionate concern as children with disabilities. The depth of this concern is reflected by the extraordinary efforts and sacrifices made by the families of these children and by the resources that society commits to them through government programs. These programs, however, tend to be in a constant state of flux, with significant changes occurring over time in participation levels, the structure of benefits, and total expenditures. Such changes tend to occur in piecemeal fashion, as a consequence of separate items of legislation, changing societal standards, evolving awareness of chronic conditions, court decisions, and maturation of public programs. At one point in time, society responds with new resources to meet new or perceived needs, at another, with fewer resources due to new budget crunches or perceptions of abuse.

Such methods of expansion or contraction are not unusual in the public policy arena, but they can entail real costs. In particular, they are seldom likely to ensure that resources are devoted to the most important needs in society or that government programs are well-coordinated or integrated. They are unlikely to be equitable or efficient in approach or even consistent in outcome.

As this study evolved, we discovered that the piecemeal nature of policy had a parallel in the community involved in disability issues, and extended to the more academic research on programs for children with disabilities. We found that few professionals had access to sources that provided a system-wide multi-program perspective. Perhaps this, too, was a natural consequence of separate attempts to respond to specific medical conditions or types of needs, before taking a broader and more integrated perspective. It may be that policy, research, and advocacy approaches reinforced each other—once programs were created, research and advocacy would center on an individual program, often in isolation. We do not mean to decry either the quality or merit of these efforts. But they tended to leave serious gaps. How does one deal with the relationships among programs?

With the relative needs of what is really a heterogenous population? With deciding whether a dollar spent to achieve some good here in this program might be better spent there in that program?

The most glaring example of the existing gap was that nowhere was there gathered in a single place a simple accounting of the combined expenditures made by programs for children with disabilities. A significant portion of this study, therefore, was designed to begin to fill that gap. This effort, in turn, gave rise to a number of related questions. What are the major ways in which the country today is responding to the needs of these children and their families? Which levels of jurisdiction—federal, state, or local—are most involved? How much assistance is provided in cash versus in the form of educational services or health care? If one is considering changes in a federal cash assistance program or in an educational benefit or a health benefit, how large or small might these changes be within the larger system of programs? What are the connections to other programs that might be affected?

As we discovered, even defining disability is a challenging task. Different programs use differing and often inconsistent diagnostic classifications, disability-related terms, and eligibility standards. Even the types of information and tools used to diagnose children differ widely. Many of these very basic but complex issues are the subject of intense examination by others, and we certainly do not resolve them here. Our more modest goal is simply to acknowledge many of these difficult issues, and to encourage more systematic thinking about how these differences affect programs individually and in combination.

Systematic thinking about these programs, however, is not achieved simply by documenting and comparing what exists. A further step is to confront the more difficult issue of how to think about making choices as to who should benefit and what types of benefits should be provided within this system of programs. Certainly we can begin by stating certain broad societal goals, such as increasing opportunity for children with disabilities and assuring their full participation in society. While such goals are necessary for thinking about this issue, they are not sufficient. The simple fact is that resources available to government and society in general are limited. Perhaps more resources can be made available for children with disabilities if some other program is cut, some other tax is raised, or the economy grows. Regardless, we cannot ignore the fundamental issue of how to allocate the resources that are available. Where wants are unlimited and resources are limited—a condition and constraint affecting almost every private and public activity—we must have a guiding set of principles for thinking about making these difficult choices.

Another major portion of this study, therefore, is devoted to providing an integrated approach or framework for examining such choices. The potential gains from using such a framework to guide a decision-making process are large. In an expanding economy, it is likely that more resources will be made available for children with disabilities—less than some would like, more than others desire. If we force ourselves to make more explicit our choices about use of these resources, it is more likely we will allocate them better than if existing programs are simply expanded at random or only in response to the greatest political pressures.

Without a systematic approach to making choices, programs are less likely to evolve in the most beneficial manner, our ability to meet needs will be reduced, and possible investments in children will be deterred—with longer-term consequences for the children themselves. We do not mean to imply that more rigorous thinking about choices will lead to easy or obvious conclusions about where to allocate resources, but it is likely to help avoid big mistakes. A major reason that even systematically deliberated choices remain difficult is that even the best of principles may conflict among each other. For instance, much spending on children with disabilities is clearly designed to serve an investment function and help these children become more self-sufficient. But like other educational expenditures, such efforts often help those with greatest potential more than those with greatest need. Principles don't tell us which is more important, they only make clearer the nature of the tradeoffs before us.

Although our focus in this study is on programs for children with disabilities, we believe that the same type of systematic thinking can be applied, with modest adaptation, to a number of other areas such as disability programs for adults and other combinations of social transfer programs.

Over the past half century, social welfare functions have displaced other functions such as defense and transportation as the major and dominant tasks of government at all levels—federal, state, and local. It is not surprising, then, that government and voters would give increased scrutiny to those activities that have become relatively more important. The state of flux with respect to programs for children with disabilities has a parallel in many other areas of social welfare. Since citizens naturally reexamine what government does, it is highly unlikely that the increased attention given to social welfare programs in general, and to programs for children with disabilities, in particular, is going to dissipate. We may as well, therefore, provide a sound analytic base for this examination, one that systematically considers interactions among programs and the relationship of principles to the choices before us. We only hope that this study provides a modest base for such systematic thinking—one on which others may be able to build.

Chapter 2 of this book provides a brief introduction to childhood disability. We review the many difficulties one encounters when trying to measure or even define childhood disability, and estimates of the number of children in the country with a disability. The chapter then turns to the system of programs available to children with disabilities, including a brief look at who these programs were designed to serve, the types of benefits or services delivered through these programs, how many children are served, and at what cost.

Chapter 3 presents a set of principles which we believe can help guide more systematic and thoughtful discussions about how best to serve children with disabilities. The chapter also illustrates how many seemingly intractable debates—such as whether benefits should be made in cash or in direct services such as education—are essentially reflections of different principles in conflict.

A program-by-program review of the largest programs serving children with disabilities today is presented in Part II of this book. That the current period is one of potentially large changes for social programs—including programs that serve children with disabilities—makes it more rather than less important to do this program-by-program review. An accounting of programs currently in place serves several functions. First, it demonstrates how policy and programs have been approached in the past. Second, it provides a benchmark against which change can be measured. Third, it documents the needs that exist—and will continue to exist regardless of whether the particular programs or administrative responsibilities shift.

For each program, we cover the eligibility requirements, how the program is administered, what benefits or services are provided, how many children participate in the program (and what have been the trends over time in participation levels), and finally expenditures on the program by the federal, state, and local governments. The information contained in Part II was gleaned from a large number of published and unpublished sources, and we hope that it will serve as a valuable resource to many members of the childhood disability community. As we discovered soon after embarking on this project, many program planners, administrators, service providers, and others sought information beyond the one or two programs with which they worked directly. Hopefully, the material provided in this section may help them in this search.

Perhaps the group most familiar with the many programs we review are the families of children with disabilities themselves. After all, it is these families who must daily navigate this complex and often uncoordinated system of programs. It is they who must piece together the various services they need to help their children develop and flourish. We hope that this book helps all of us gain some perspective on the enormity of that task.

Chapter Two

PROGRAMS FOR CHILDREN WITH DISABILITIES: AN OVERVIEW

Children with disabilities are served by many public programs run by federal, state, and local governments, such as special education, Medicaid, and Supplemental Security Income (SSI). These programs are interrelated, even though often not coordinated. To be understood comprehensively, they must be considered together. That is the purpose of this chapter.

We proceed in two major steps. First, we investigate some of the difficult problems in defining disability and then, based upon some different definitions, provide some rough estimates of the prevalence of childhood disability. We then examine major government programs serving children with disabilities and provide estimates of the coverage and the total amount of funding of each program. Along the way we give due recognition to the many private efforts and costs that are not reflected in government programs. Although these costs have never been estimated in aggregate, public programs operate best when they are at least coordinated with, and take account of, these private efforts.

DEFINING AND MEASURING CHILDHOOD DISABILITY

Childhood disabilities are defined and measured in many different ways depending on the purposes and needs of service providers, program planners and administrators, researchers, and policymakers. School district officials responsible for projecting the need for special education teachers, for example, want to know how many children have certain types of physical, emotional, or cognitive disability while city planners concerned with designing accessible public buildings and facilities will be interested in the number of children with different types of mobility limitations. Similarly, programs serving children with disabilities rely on different operational definitions of disability depending on what types of benefits or services the program provides and to whom.[1] Ideally, sources of information on children's disabilities should be able to support broad definitions that can be tailored to a variety of more specific purposes.[2]

Estimates of the numbers of children with disabilities are based on different types of information.[3] One common approach has been to use data on the prevalence of disabling chronic *conditions*. This method is clearly quite appropriate for measuring the prevalence of specific disabling conditions of interest, such as autism or cerebral palsy. Using chronic conditions to measure the prevalence of disability more generally, however, requires that one decide what (lists of) conditions are included in a given measure, and what are the criteria for condition *duration* and *severity*. Large-scale surveys and smaller clinical studies typically rely on lists of diagnoses to determine if a respondent has a chronic condition. A common duration criterion is used in the National Health Interview Survey (NHIS): a condition is considered chronic if it has an actual or expected duration of 3 months or longer. It is also important to consider the severity of a condition. Not all chronic conditions are disabling. To isolate those chronic disabling conditions that result in an activity limitation, for example, one should exclude very mild conditions (such as a mild allergy) or conditions that do not have a substantial impact on the physical, mental, or psychosocial life of a child (such as hypertension). A condition's severity has typically been measured by any of several functional criteria or by the need for extraordinary medical attention. In the National Health Interview Survey, for example, a limitation of activity criterion is used to determine the presence of a chronic condition.

The sensitivity of prevalence measures to the chronic conditions included and how severity is measured is illustrated in Table 2.1. Drawing on a single data source alone—the 1988 NHIS—various studies estimate the proportion of American children with one or more chronic conditions to range from around 5 percent to more than 30 percent. Most of these children have only a "mild" or "moderate" condition (such as a mild allergy or skin conditions) that is unlikely to result in a disability or activity limitation. The NHIS data suggest that around 5 percent of children have a chronic condition that is disabling. More recent results from the 1993 NHIS indicate that 4.4 million children under the age of 18, or 6.6 percent of all children in this age group, are reported to have some degree of limitation of activity.[4]

Table 2.1 PREVALENCE OF CHILDREN WITH CHRONIC HEALTH CONDITIONS: RESULTS FROM THE NATIONAL HEALTH INTERVIEW SURVEY

Source:	Severe	Mod-erate	Mild	Total	Survey	N	Popu-lation
1. Newacheck & Stoddard, 1994	1%	3%	15%	19%	NHIS, 1988	17,110	< 18
2. Newacheck & Taylor, 1992	2%	9%	20%	31%	NHIS, 1988	17,110	< 18
3. Newacheck et al., 1991	3%	7%	21%	32%	NHIS, 1988	7,465	10–17
4. Gortmaker et al., 1990				9%	NHIS, 1981	11,699	4–17
5. Newacheck, 1989	.5%	4%	2%	6%	NHIS, 1988	15,181	10–17

Comments:

1. Defined chronic conditions as one of 17 condition groups listed in the NHIS (the checklist method). Levels of severity correspond to 1, 2, or 3 or more conditions.
2. Defined chronic conditions as one of 19 condition groups listed in the NHIS (the checklist method). Defined severity as extent of "bother" and degree of limitation in daily activities.
3. Defined chronic conditions as one of 19 condition groups listed in the NHIS (the checklist method). Levels of severity correspond to 1, 2, or 3 or more conditions.
4. Defined chronic conditions using checklist method.
5. Defined population as limited in activities. Mild is limited in nonmajor activities; moderate is limited in kind or amount of major activity; severe is unable to conduct major activity.

Sources: Henry T. Ireys and Susan Shapiro Gross, "Curriculum on Children with Special Health Care Needs and Their Families," Department of Maternal and Child Health, School of Hygiene and Public Health, The Johns Hopkins University, Baltimore, MD, April 1994.
Paul W. Newacheck and Jeffrey J. Stoddard, "Prevalence and Impact of Multiple Childhood Chronic Illnesses," *Journal of Pediatrics*, Vol. 124, No. 1, January 1994.

While closely related, a chronic condition is not the same as having a disability. The term disability typically refers to the presence of some type of functional limitation. Although a child may have the same underlying chronic condition, the disability that results from this condition may change dramatically over time. Some advocates and other interested parties in the disability community are trying to discourage the use of categorical (or condition-specific) approaches to measuring disability. Instead, they support a noncategorical or functional approach. The U.S. Supreme Court's February 1990 decision in *Sullivan v. Zebley* in part reflects such a shift. This decision required that the Social Security Administration use an approach that brought the children's eligibility determination process in line with that of adults. To comply, SSA added to its established SSI process for children (which until that point had consisted of a list of specific medical conditions needed to qualify a child as "disabled") a method for assessing a child's functioning in five areas *(without regard to specific condition)*: cognition, communication, motor abilities, social abilities, and patterns of interaction.

Several conceptual frameworks have been developed to systematically describe and organize many disability-related terms (e.g., injury, impairment, chronic condition, functional limitation). A widely used framework is the "functional limitation" or Nagi framework, named after Saad Nagi.[5] Four basic concepts underlie Nagi's framework: pathology, impairment, functional limitation, and disability.[6]

The first concept, pathology, refers to the effects at the cellular and tissue level of agents such as disease, infection, trauma, congenital condition, or metabolic imbalance. Impairments refer to the loss or abnormality of mental, physical, or biochemical functions, which interfere with the normal functioning of organs or organ systems (as distinct from the organism as a whole). While all pathologies result in some type of impairment, a given impairment may be caused by different pathologies. Examples of impairments include the absence of a limb or body part, mechanical problems with joints, reduced blood flow, etc. The third concept, functional limitation, refers to the effects of impairments on the performance or performance capacity of an individual. Although both impairments and functional limitations involve the concept of *function*, functional limitations are manifested at the level of the organism as a whole (rather than molecules, cells, tissues, organs, etc.). While all functional limitations are caused by some type (or combination) of impairment, not all impairments result in functional limitations. Examples of functional limitations are an inability to lift a heavy weight or to walk a certain distance.

The final concept underlying Nagi's disability framework is the term disability itself. Nagi defines this term as the expression of a physical or mental limitation within a specific social or environmental context. While functional limitations characterize organismic functioning, disability characterizes social functioning.[7] Thus, according to Nagi, disability is a limited ability (or inability) to perform socially-defined roles and tasks within a specific sociocultural or physical environment. This definition focuses on the outcome of the *interaction* between impairments/functional limitations and behavioral/performance expectations of socially-defined roles.

The importance of considering factors *external* to the person with disabilities is illustrated by Nagi's discussion of the factors which shape the nature and severity of an individual's disabilities:

(a) the individual's definition of the situation and reactions, which at times compound the limitations; (b) the definition of the situation by others, and their reactions and expectations—especially those who are significant in the lives of the person with the disabling condition (e.g., family members, friends and associates, employers and co-workers, and organizations and professions that provide services and benefits); and (c) characteristics of the environment and the degree to which it is free from, or encumbered with, physical and sociocultural barriers.[8]

A number of researchers have questioned the applicability of Nagi's framework to mental and emotional conditions. In general, these arguments have stemmed from the assertion that mental and emotional conditions are by their nature more socially grounded than are physiological and anatomical conditions, and further, that (with the exception of conditions that are organic in origin) current knowledge does not permit a clear distinction between pathology, impairment, and functional limitation in the case of mental and emotional conditions. In the psychiatric literature a distinction is often made between "organic" and "functional" disorders, the latter reflecting the need to infer from the level of functional limitations, the pathology and impairment associated with a given mental or emotional condition. Nagi has argued, however, that "distinctions between indicators of functional limitations and those of disability *can* be established with sufficient clarity. Intelligence tests, scales of psychophysiological reactions, other psychometric tests, and clinical assessments have been used to identify functional limitations independent of whether, and to what extent, a person is limited in performing expected roles and tasks."[9]

Diagnostic Definitions, Classifications, and Ways of Determining Eligibility[10]

In practice, no single definitional or classification system has been used by service providers or others in the childhood disability community. Differences in the way children with disabilities are diagnosed and classified remain a continuing problem that affects choices in medical, educational, social, and rehabilitative services. These differences complicate decisions about eligibility, transitioning across programs, program funding, and documentation of program impact. For researchers and policymakers, it also adds to the difficulty of comparing studies and systematically analyzing different policies. This variability reflects conceptual, semantic, and measurement issues and manifests itself in a number of important areas that are briefly reviewed below.

Given a child's profile of disabilities, the way in which that child is classified may vary depending on the agency or entity responsible for providing services. In special education services, for example, a child with the same underlying conditions may be assigned a diagnosis of behaviorally-emotionally handicapped (BEH), severely emotionally disturbed (SED), or behavior disordered (BD). If this same child sees a mental health professional, psychiatric diagnoses (DSM IV) such as mood disorder or conduct disorder are likely to be assigned.[11] Variations such as these are not only found among different service agencies, but also among many professional organizations. The official definition of mental retardation as advanced by the American Association of Mental Retardation, for instance, differs from definitions used in special education and rehabilitation services. Other professional organizations such as the National Society for Autistic Children and the Association on Learning Disabilities also have diagnostic criteria which are specific to autism and learning disabilities, respectively.

In spite of the passage of two major legislative acts emphasizing the appropriateness of the term "disabilities" (the Americans with Disabilities Act and the Individuals with Disabilities Education Act), alternative terms are constantly used. When the adjective "visual" is combined with any of the terms "disorder," "impairment," "deficit," or "handicap," the same meaning is implied. That these terms are not conceptually or semantically equivalent has been the basis for the differentiated taxonomy developed for the International Classification of Impairments, Disabilities, and Handicap (ICIDH). A related problem is that terms used to describe a condition's severity such as "mild," "moderate," "severe," or "profound" may mean something quite different depending upon the underlying condition (e.g., auditory versus mental impairment) and the operational or functional task being examined (e.g., ability to hear, ability to function in society on one's own).

A comparison of three major pieces of legislation clearly illustrates this type of variability. Legislation for infants and toddlers (P.L. 99-457) defines eligible populations on the basis of functional limitations in one or more developmental areas (physical, cognitive, language, social, and self-help). A different set of functional limitations (e.g., independent living, mobility, etc.) serves as the basis for defining disability in adolescents and adults (P.L. 95-602). The law establishing special education services for school-age children (P.L. 94-142), on the other hand, defines eligible children according to ten or more diagnostic categories such as mental retardation, visual impairment, or learning disabilities. In special education services, there may be differences among states not only in the number of categories, but in the nature of the criteria used to assign individuals to a particular category. As a result, a child's eligibility for special education services may change simply by moving from one state to another.

Differing types of information are used to diagnose and classify children with disabilities. The criteria for mental retardation and learning disabilities, for example, are based on psychometric evidence in the form of individual test scores. Assignment to the categories of visual, auditory, or motor impairment is based on biomedical or re- lated criteria. The categories of emotional or behavioral disorders, by contrast, are typically based on clinical judgment. These assorted sources of variability contribute to the substantial differences from one state to another in the number of children receiving special ed- ucation and related services. These problems also make it difficult to provide sustained services to children. In the transition from early intervention to pre-school services, the shift from non-categorical to categorical eligibility has resulted in almost one-third of previously eligible children losing eligibility.[12] Another consequence of the cat- egorical approach is substantial instability of assignment—one study showed that about 25 percent of students had two or more classifica- tions during their years of special education attendance.[13]

Diagnoses and classifications may be further complicated by age, situation, and measurement tools chosen. "Developmental delay" is a diagnosis that defines eligibility for services in infant and pre-school programs. It is not, however, a diagnostic category for children of school age. Learning disability is typically defined in terms of a dis- crepancy between ability and academic achievement and is not likely to be assigned to a young preschooler. The role of "situational con- text," in turn, has long been an issue, as the classification of children as mentally retarded has led to the disproportionate assignment of this label to minority and disadvantaged children. This concern has led to various modifications in eligibility determination, including the prohibition of standardized intelligence testing of minority chil- dren in some states. Measurement tools also affect classification. Cen- tral to the diagnosis of learning disability, for instance, is discrepancy from standard scores for ability and achievement. The size and nature of this discrepancy is clearly a function of the properties (statistical, learning functions examined, etc.) of the test used to determine eli- gibility. Appropriate quantitative measurement has also proven difficult in classifying the growing categorical group of children with attention deficit disorders.

Two classification issues remain. While children may be assigned to different categories because of different conditions, children who are classified differently may in fact have quite similar functional characteristics. Children who have different labels may have as much in common as children who share the same label. Alternatively, the different types of issues faced by a defined categorical group may overlap with those of other categorical groups. This is further complicated by the co-occurrence of two or more disabilities in one child (who may be labeled with a single disability or with multiple disabilities). Increasing recognition of these types of complexities has contributed to proposals for assessing children with disabilities and chronic illness[14] according to functional limitations (e.g., eating, mobility, etc.) rather than determining eligibility and providing services on the basis of categories that only loosely relate to functional abilities.[15]

MEASURING NEEDS

A major limitation of existing diagnostic and classification approaches is that they do not provide an adequate basis for determining the service needs of a child. The taxonomic approaches used in medicine (ICD-10) and mental health (DSM-IV) and the categorical system used for special education have focused on etiology (e.g., traumatic brain injury), manifested impairment (e.g., visual), or a construct (e.g., learning disability, attention deficit disorder). Given the prescriptive limitations of diagnostic categories, the prevailing practice in early intervention, special education, and related habilitative services for children has been to formulate individualized service plans (e.g., IFSP, IEP) relative to the child's age and the setting providing services. The assessment data on which these individualized plans are based, however, often do not adequately capture individual and family characteristics that are important for planning, providing, and evaluating services.

Many social service programs must project demand, allocate resources, and document cost-effectiveness. Meeting this challenge requires summary measures which efficiently capture the nature and extent of children's needs. In response, there has been a growing interest in understanding how functional assessments (first developed in the fields of medicine and rehabilitation) can be applied to other areas. In general terms, functional assessments by-pass the medically-specialized levels of etiology and diagnosis, and focus instead on the documentation of basic functioning (e.g., mobility, speech, etc.). Often it takes the form of ordinal ratings made by someone knowledgeable about the person with a disability.[16]

A desirable feature of any summary measure is to account for the needs of a child with a given profile of disabilities. "Burden of illness" summary measures have been productively explored in medical and psychiatric contexts. One study of length of hospital stays found them to be strongly related to a functional index of illness severity (the Computerized Severity Index). In a related study in a psychiatric setting, a similar severity index was found to differentially account for outcomes of hospitalization as a function of primary diagnosis. In the fields of geriatrics and rehabilitation, the concept of "burden of care" has been suggested as a way of summarizing the combined needs of an individual with a chronic condition relative to the demand for services and other resources. As service plans and program evaluations in these fields become more sophisticated, more formal techniques and analyses of the burden of care concept are emerging.[17]

The use of summary measures has also been extended to studies of families with children with multiple disabilities and chronic illness.[18] An important consideration in the usefulness of such measures is that they account for the significant role of different functions.[19] The aggregated index of disability unique to a given child should take into account financial burdens of care, time costs for caregivers, and related measures of care-load for service systems.[20] Because children have varying profiles of disability, summary indices must be sensitive to both conditions and intensity. Two children with similar disabilities but different intensities should yield different weighted burden of care indices. Such weighted indices of burden of care would be useful to develop and test in the future as one means to (try to) enhance the sensitivity of program evaluation and policy analysis to the needs for services by children with disabilities. To what extent these burden of care indices can be adopted by programs serving children with disabilities remains to be seen.

PREVALENCE OF DISABILITY AMONG CHILDREN

Despite the many problems associated with defining and measuring the population of children with disabilities, estimates of the total number of these children are needed and have been developed. One recent analysis estimated that there are 4.5 million children with a disability in the U.S (see Table 2.2).[21] This estimate is in part derived from the Survey of Income and Program Participation (or SIPP) and uses reports of limitations in age-appropriate functional activities as a basis for identifying persons with disabilities. Few children with disabilities live in institutions: an estimated 1,200 live in nursing homes, 29,500 are in facilities for people with mental illness, 1,100 live in homes for people with physical handicaps, and 60,000 reside in facilities serving those with mental retardation. Several sources indicate that the prevalence of disabilities among children and adolescents has been increasing over time. The exact cause of these increases is not known, but possible reasons include changes in how data are collected, increased survivorship among low birth weight infants and children with terminal chronic illnesses (due to advances in medical technology), improved responsiveness to programs that assist individuals identified as having a disability, and finally, greater awareness and detection by parents, educators, and health care professionals. This last factor may explain the very large increase in the numbers of children diagnosed with learning disabilities.[22]

The 1991 SIPP data also suggest that while 6 percent of all children under the age of 17 have some type of disability, less than 1.5 percent have a severe disability (see Table 2.3). The proportion of children identified as having a disability (or a severe disability) increases dramatically with the age of the child. Furthermore, as children age, the

Table 2.2 COMMUNITY AND INSTITUTIONAL STATUS OF CHILDREN UNDER AGE 18 WITH DISABILITIES: 1990 (IN THOUSANDS)

	Total
Total	4,536.3
Community	4,444.5
Institutions and Group Quarters	91.8
Nursing Homes	1.2
Facilities for the Mentally Ill	29.5
Homes for the Physically Handicapped	1.1
Facilities for the Mentally Retarded	60.0
Intermediate-Care Facilities for the Mentally Retarded	20.0
Other Mentally Retarded Facilities	26.0
Child Welfare/Foster Care for Mentally Retarded Children	14.0

Source of Data: 1990 SIPP; 1990 Decennial Census; Unpublished data, Center for Mental Health Statistics (DHHS); Unpublished data, Lakin (University of Minnesota).
Source: Michele Adler, "Disability Among Children," *ASPE Research Notes*, U.S. Department of Health and Human Services, January 1995.

Table 2.3 DISABILITY STATUS OF CHILDREN 0 TO 17 YEARS OLD, BY AGE, SEX, AND RACE AND HISPANIC ORIGIN: 1991–92

Age	All Children Percent with a: Disability	Severe Disability	Males Percent with a: Disability	Severe Disability	Females Percent with a: Disability	Severe Disability
Under 3 years	2.2	0.4	2.2	0.5	2.1	0.1
3 to 5 years	5.2	0.7	6.2	0.9	4.1	0.4
6 to 14 years	6.3	1.3	8.2	1.5	4.3	1.0
15 to 17 years	9.3	3.1	10.8	3.1	7.7	3.1
Total Under 18	5.8	1.3	7.2	1.5	4.4	1.1

Age	White Percent with a: Disability	Severe Disability	Black Percent with a: Disability	Severe Disability	Hispanic Origin Percent with a: Disability	Severe Disability
Under 3 years	2.2	0.3	2.5	0.5	1.2	0.2
3 to 5 years	5.5	0.7	4.3	0.4	2.5	0.2
6 to 14 years	6.5	1.4	5.9	0.8	4.1	0.6
15 to 17 years	8.9	2.6	10.9	5.5	8.5	2.3
Total Under 18	5.9	1.3	5.8	1.5	4.0	0.7

Source of Data: 1990 and 1991 Survey of Income and Program Participation (SIPP). Source: John M. McNeil, *Americans with Disabilities: 1991–92*, U.S. Bureau of the Census, Current Population Reports, P70-33, U.S. Government Printing Office, Washington, D.C., 1993.

proportion of boys with a disability increasingly exceeds the corresponding proportion for girls of the same age. Thus, while the percentage of children under three with a disability is virtually the same for boys and girls (just over 2 percent), by the time they reach age 15 to 17, close to 11 percent of boys are reported to have a disability, compared to less than 8 percent of girls. There are also racial and ethnic differences in the proportion of children in different age groups who have a disability. At the youngest (under 3 years of age) and older (ages 15 to 17) ages, black children are more likely than other children to have both a disability and a severe disability. For the middle age groups (3 to 5 years and 6 to 14 years), the highest share of disability and severe disability is reported among white children. Interestingly, Hispanic children (who may be of either race) of all ages were less likely than both their black and white counterparts to report having either a disability or a severe disability.

The most common conditions identified as the cause of a child's disability are shown in Table 2.4 (note that these are conditions causing any disability, not just severe disabilities). By far the most commonly reported conditions are learning disabilities, accounting for almost one-third of all conditions reported. Other relatively common conditions are speech problems (13 percent), mental retardation (7 percent), asthma (6 percent), and mental or emotional problems.

It is important to keep in mind that very few estimates of childhood disability (including the ones we present here) encompass reliable measures of the number of children in need of mental health services.[23] After an extensive review of existing studies, the Office of Technology Assessment concluded:

Table 2.4 CONDITIONS REPORTED AS CAUSE OF DISABILITY,
          CHILDREN 0 TO 17 YEARS OLD: 1991–92

Condition (first, second, or third condition)	Number	Percent Distribution
TOTAL	4,858	100.0
Asthma	311	6.4
Autism	48	1.0
Blindness or vision problems	144	3.0
Cancer	26	0.5
Cerebral Palsy	129	2.7
Deafness or serious trouble hearing	116	2.4
Diabetes	14	0.3
Drug or alcohol problem or disorder	48	1.0
Epilepsy or seizure disorder	128	2.6
Hay fever or other respiratory allergies	76	1.6
Head or spinal cord injury	45	0.9
Heart trouble	44	0.9
Impairment or deformity of back, side, foot, or leg	121	2.5
Impairment or deformity of finger, hand, or arm	27	0.6
Learning disability	1,435	29.5
Mental or emotional problem or disorder	305	6.3
Mental retardation	331	6.8
Missing legs, feet, toes, arms, hands, or fingers	70	1.4
Paralysis of any kind	73	1.5
Speech problems	634	13.1
Tonsillitis or repeated ear infections	80	1.6
Other	653	13.4

Note: Table figures refer to conditions, not children. A child may have more than one of the conditions listed.
Source of Data: 1990 and 1991 Survey of Income and Program Participation.
Source: John M. McNeil, Americans with Disabilities: 1991–92, U.S. Bureau of the Census, Current Population Reports, P70-33, U.S. Government Printing Office, Washington, D.C., 1993.

There appears to be a significant gap between the number of children identified in epidemiologic assessments as requiring mental health services and the number receiving services. There is general agreement that at least 12 percent of the nation's children—7.5 million—are in need of some type of mental health treatment. Available evidence suggests that only a small number (fewer than one-third) of the children who have mental health problems receive treatment. An unknown number of children may be at risk for mental health problems and in need of preventive services.[24]

SIZE AND SCOPE OF PROGRAMS SERVING CHILDREN WITH DISABILITIES

Various estimates of the exact number of children with disabilities all confirm that there are many children and families with special needs. Children with disabilities and their families are served through public programs designed to meet a variety of needs: including educational, economic, medical, and developmental. The exact mix of programs in which any given child or family participates depends on the needs of the child and family, the family's economic and social resources, and how programs identify and serve these children.

Since a detailed documentation of all programs serving children with disabilities is beyond the scope of this study, we concentrate on the largest programs which have a direct focus on children with disabilities: Supplemental Security Income (SSI), Medicaid, Parts B and H of the Individuals with Disabilities Education Act (IDEA), Maternal and Child Health Block Grants, state mental retardation/developmental disability programs (MR/DD), state mental health programs, Head Start, and state family support programs. Many other programs serve children with disabilities, but most do not have disability eligibility criteria. Examples of these include Food Stamps, Aid to Families with Dependent Children, foster care and child welfare programs, and housing subsidies. We do not examine these programs here because we often cannot separate out expenditures for children with disabilities and because these programs would be available to children regardless of their disability status. Still other programs serving children with disabilities are not included because they are small in size or, like Vocational Rehabilitation, they focus mainly on the transition to adulthood.

An extensive review of each of these programs can be found in Chapter 4 of Part II. Here we provide an overview of the major aspects of these programs so that we start with a picture of the entire system and how programs differ and relate to each other and the whole. Table 2.5 contains a snapshot of the programs we review later, including program mission, a brief statement of eligibility, participation levels, federal, state, and local expenditures, major service or benefit provided, and primary administrative level.

The two major federal programs for children with disabilities are SSI, which provides cash benefits, and Medicaid, which provides medical benefits. These two programs account for approximately two-thirds of all federal spending on children with disabilities among the programs we review. Both of these federal programs are means-tested programs; they provide benefits mainly to children with disabilities in low-income families.

Cash benefits from SSI can be used by the child's family for food, shelter, or almost anything that benefits the child, but are not limited to disability-related needs. Large increases in participation since 1990 (over 250 percent) have led to increased scrutiny of the purposes and disability eligibility criteria of the SSI program. Several recent proposals have been made attempting to restrain this rate of growth. Two important reasons for increases in the program are changes in eligibility due to the Supreme Court *Zebley v. Sullivan* decision and changes in mental impairment listings, and increased outreach activities. Federal expenditures in 1993 were over $4 billion and state expenditures supplementing these benefits were $200 million. Almost 900,000 children were receiving SSI at the end of 1994.

Medicaid for the most part operates as a basic health insurance plan for low-income families. In most states, children receiving SSI are eligible for benefits, although there are a variety of ways children with disabilities can become eligible. In addition to services commonly covered by insurers, Medicaid also covers expenses of residential care facilities for certain children with disabilities, including long-term care for persons with mental retardation and developmental disabilities. Increasingly, Medicaid funds are used to finance community-based services, MR/DD programs, and services provided through the special education system. Medicaid is a federal matching program, where the federal government matches state expenditures at a rate determined by formula. In 1993, Medicaid covered almost 800,000 children with disabilities.[25] The federal government spent $3.4 billion and state governments spent $2.5 billion. State Medicaid expenditures are the second largest share of state expenditures for children with disabilities.

The largest program for children with disabilities in terms of both expenditures and participation levels is special education. Special education and support services for children with disabilities are administered, financed, and delivered at the state and local levels. Part B of the Individuals with Disabilities Education Act (IDEA) assures all children with disabilities "a free appropriate public education," and grant-in-aid funding is provided to support elementary and secondary education services. States are required to serve children (aged 5 to 21) and preschoolers (aged 3 to 5) with disabilities. Through special education programs, schools effectively deliver to school-age children with disabilities a wide variety of "related services" other than education. These services include speech pathology, psychological services, counseling, physical therapy, and some diagnostic medical services. In the 1992–93 school year, about 5 million children (more than six times the number of children receiving SSI) received special education services. The majority of funding for special education comes from state and local governments. In 1992–93, almost $2.5 billion in federal funds and an estimated $29 billion in state and local government funds were spent on special education and related services. Unlike the major federal programs for children with disabilities, special education programs are open to families at all income levels.

A variety of other programs provide services specifically to children with disabilities. These include Part H Early Intervention services, the state Title V Children with Special Health Care Needs program, state mental retardation and developmental disabilities programs, state mental health agency programs, and Head Start. For the most part these are administered at the state and local levels. The federal government's involvement is through the provision of block grants or targeted grants, allowing Medicaid to finance some programs, and varying levels of regulatory oversight. With the exception of Head Start, all of these programs are primarily funded by states.

- Part H of IDEA supports early intervention programs for children from birth through two years of age. It provides for remedial or preventive services for children with developmental delays or conditions causing delays. Part H Early Intervention services were delivered to almost 144,000 infants and toddlers in 1993 at a federal cost of $213 million and state cost of $328 million.
- Title V MCH Block Grants pay for public health functions (e.g., needs assessment, planning, and coordination with other programs), and population-based services (e.g., newborn screenings,

Table 2.5 OVERVIEW OF MAJOR PROGRAMS SERVING CHILDREN WITH
DISABILITIES

Program	Program Mission	Eligibility
Supplemental Security Income (SSI)[a]	To provide "special assistance in order to help [recipients] become self-supporting members of our society."	Meet disability and low-income criteria.
Medicaid[b] Intermediate Care Facilities/MR Inpatient Psychiatric Nursing Facilities	To provide basic health insurance and financing for long-term medical and social services programs.	SSI recipient (generally), low-income and (a) high medical bills, (b) AFDC recipient, or (c) reside in certain MR/DD care facilities.
Special Education[c] Section 611, Part B, IDEA Section 619, Part B, IDEA (Preschool) Chapter 1 (SOP)	"To assure that all children with disabilities have available to them . . . a free *appropriate* public education which emphasizes special education and related services designed to meet their unique needs . . ." [IDEA]	Children from 3 to 21 years; broad federal guidelines for categorical disability criteria (specific assessment tools determined locally); no financial criteria.
Part H Early Intervention Services[d]	To minimize (and perhaps preclude) later need for special education services or institutionalization.	Children from birth to 3 years who manifest developmental delays or condition likely to cause delay (states refine).
Title V, Children with Special Health Care Needs (CSHCN) Program[e]	To improve the health of *all* mothers and children consistent with state and national health objectives (Title V).	States establish own financial and medical eligibility criteria.
Programs for Mental Retardation/Developmental Disabilities (MR/DD)[f] Administration on DD State MR/DD Programs Large Residential Services Community Services	To "empower individuals with disabilities to maximize employment, economic self-sufficiency, independence, and inclusion and integration into society." [Rehabilitation Act of 1973]	Children and adults with developmental disabilities.
Mental Health Programs[g] Center for Mental Health Services State Mental Health Agencies	To "provide a broad array of mental health services that are community-based and family-centered" [program goals statement of the CMHS Child Mental Health Services Initiative].	Children with a variety of conditions including substance abuse, serious emotional disturbance, or other related conditions that limit functioning at home, school, or in the community.
Head Start[h]	To strengthen the ability of disadvantaged children to succeed in school and in later life.	Family income below poverty or receive AFDC (generally); at least 10 percent of all slots must meet disability criteria.
Total	—	—

Table 2.5 OVERVIEW OF MAJOR PROGRAMS SERVING CHILDREN WITH DISABILITIES

Number of Children Served Annually	Unduplicated Annual Expenditures on Children (in million $)		Main Service or Benefit [Primary Level of Administration]
	Federal	State/Local	
766,740	4,082	202	Cash benefits. [Federal]
796,279	3,395	2,459	Medical expenses, long-term and intermediate care facility ex-
12,526	395	286	penses (includes room and
51,470	607	439	board), and community/family
5,506	124	90	support services. [Federal/State]
4,452,117	2,046	17,714 (state)	Specially designed instruction
441,748	326	11,415 (local)	meeting the unique needs of
199,928	126		child with disability; related services such as transportation, and developmental, corrective, and other supportive services needed to benefit from special education. [State/Local]
143,392	213	328	Remedial (or preventive) services for children with developmental delays or conditions causing delays. [State/Local]
755,000	155	221	Enabling or wrap-around, disease-specific, and basic medical services. [State]
Unknown	115	N/A	State demonstration grants, pro-
Unknown	9	85	tection, advocacy, and research.
	23	345	[State]
			Institutions, large and small residential services, and community services (e.g., personal assistance, family support, early intervention services).
Unknown	60	N/A	Grants for comprehensive com-
145,000	73	917	munity MH services for children/adolescents with serious emotional disturbances. [State]
			State mental hospitals, residential treatment centers, ambulatory services and community-based services.
94,235	92	23	Educational, medical, nutritional, dental, mental health, other social services. [Federal/ Local grantee]
No Unduplicative Estimate Possible	10,600	33,709	

NOTES TO TABLE 2.5

Note: Please refer to the discussion of each of these programs in Part II for sources and more detailed program information. Unless otherwise noted, figures are for FY 1993. Programs (e.g., Food Stamps) that serve children irrespective of disability status are not included. To the extent possible, expenditures represent unduplicated spending. Since many programs use Medicaid as a source of funding, attempts were made to report non-Medicaid funding for state MR/DD programs and SMHAs. Total funding for adults and children including Medicaid for MR/DD programs is $17,227 million (67 percent from Medicaid) in 1992 and for SMHAs is $12,198 million (16 percent from Medicaid) in 1990. *See page 36 for a complete list of references for Table 2.5.*

a. SSI: Social Security Annual Statistical Supplement (1994). Annualized from December 1993 data. Includes retroactive payments to children found eligible through rede-terminations after Zebley decision. Number of children served is for December 1993. Eligibility: a child under the age of 18 must have a medically determinable physical or mental impairment of comparable severity to the standard for adults (being unable to engage in any substantial gainful activity by reason of any medically determined physical or mental impairment which can be expected to result in death or which has lasted or can be expected to last for a continuous period of not less than 12 months). As of January 1995, the general financial criterion is that the child's monthly income plus income deemed from parents (less allowable exclusions and deductions) not exceed $458.

b. Medicaid: Urban Institute calculations using HCFA Forms 2082 and 64. Federal/state split uses a 58 percent federal match (a weighted average across states). Numbers exclude Arizona and Rhode Island. Total numbers reported are for children under 21 categorized as blind or disabled by states, which for the most part includes only children who are eligible through SSI receipt or receiving institutional services. Subset numbers are for children receiving each service type and are included in total. These numbers are likely undercounts, because there are children with disabilities who are not eligible for SSI but are covered by Medicaid. Total children served reflects enrollees regardless of Medicaid use while subset figures are children actually receiving services.

c. Special Education: U.S. Department of Education (1994). Data for 1992–93 school year. Numbers of children served are point in time (not annual) counts. Eligibility: "Children with disabilities" are children evaluated as having mental retardation, hearing impairments including deafness, speech or language impairments, visual impairments including blindness, serious emotional disturbance, orthopedic impairments, autism, traumatic brain injury, other health impairments, specific learning disabilities, deaf-blindness, or multiple disabilities, and who because of those impairments need special education and related services. For children aged 3 through 5, states have the option of also including children who are experiencing developmental delays (in physical development, cognitive development, communication development, social or emotional development, or adaptive development) and who because of those developmental delays need special education and related services. Section 611, Part B, IDEA: basis of formula for federal allocation includes number of preschoolers (age 3–5) in state; number of children reflects ages 6 and older only. Chapter 1 (SOP) covers children from birth through age 21. Number served reflects only those ages 3 and older, including 18,371 preschoolers (age 3–5). The 76,449 infants and toddlers (age 0–2) served under Chapter 1 (SOP) are included among those receiving Part H Early Intervention services. State and local special education figures are estimated by assuming that the distribution of special education expenditures by federal, state, and local sources is the same as that reported by states for the 1987–88 school year (the last year such data were collected from states). Known federal special education expenditures for the 1992–93 school year are used to calculate federal, state, and local shares of 7.8 percent, 56.0 percent, and 36.1 percent, respectively. Note that the state and local estimates are for all special education programs (Part B, Part B Preschool, and Chapter 1).

d. Part H Early Intervention Services: U.S. Department of Education (1994). Federal expenditures are primarily for planning, coordination, and implementation activities. Part H EI services are funded by many sources including Medicaid, Chapter 1, MCH and Child Care Block Grants, state appropriations, and private medical insurance. Based on 1989–90 data, Tom Coakley, the Technical Assistance Coordinator of NEC*TAS, estimates that federal and state Part H allocations account for approximately 13 and 20 percent, respectively, of total Part H expenditures. Using the federal FY 1993 allocation as a base, the state/local figure is derived based on this estimate. Eligibility: the Part H statute requires that each jurisdiction define more precisely the term "developmentally delayed" for determining eligibility of infants and toddlers for services under the state's program. As a result, the population of children eligible for Part H services differs considerably from one state to the next.

e. Title V CSHCN Program: Maternal and Child Health Bureau (January 1995). Data for FY 1991. Federal figure is 31 percent of total federal Title V allocations to states ($499.2 million). State/local estimate *assumes* same proportion applies for total state/local Title V expenditures ($713.9 million).

f. MR/DD programs: Administration for Developmental Disabilities expenditures from 1994 budget. Children cannot be separated, so figure not included in total. State program data from Braddock, Hemp, Bechelder, Fujiura (1994) for 1992. Child expenditures exclude Medicaid and SSI funds to avoid duplication. Expenditures for children are estimated as 8 percent of total expenditures (8 percent of persons in intermediate care facilities for mental retardation are children). This is meant to be only a rough approximation, especially for community services. Large residential services are facilities with 16 or more beds. Number of children served is not known.

g. Mental Health Programs: CMHS figures are from 1994 budget for Child Mental Health Services Initiatives only. SMHA's data are for FY 1990 from Center for Mental Health Services (1992). Child expenditures for under 18 years old are calculated as 10 percent of total expenditures using estimates from NASMHPD (1993). Since 48 percent of total SMHA spending is not allocated by age, this 10 percent number is only a rough approximation. Number of children served is from Hoagwood and Rupp (1994) for December 1988. Includes 25,000 children receiving residential services and 120,000 receiving out-patient or partial services.

h. Head Start: Head Start Bureau estimates that 3.3 percent of all program expenditures are devoted to additional services for children with disabilities. Local/state refers to "grantee" match which may be in-kind. Eligibility: the Head Start program has established specific diagnostic criteria for children with disabilities. To be counted as disabled in Head Start, children must be professionally diagnosed as having one of several disabling conditions and because of this condition, require special education and related services. Disabling conditions are blindness, visual impairment/disability, deafness, hearing impairment/disability, physical disability (orthopedic disability), speech impairment (communication disorder), health impairment, mental retardation, serious emotional disturbance, or specific learning disabilities. Children must be diagnosed by "appropriate professionals who work with children with these conditions and have certification and/or licensure to make these diagnoses."

immunization, lead poisoning prevention, outreach, and public education). MCH Block Grants also fund the Children with Special Health Care Needs (CSHCN) program, which provides children with enabling services (such as case management, health education, transportation, translation, and nutrition) and basic personal health services. In FY 1991, 755,000 children were served by the CSHCN program at an estimated cost of $376 million. Over half of the funding for this program is from state sources.

• State MR/DD and mental health programs are primarily state run and funded. Many services are funded through federal and state Medicaid expenditures. MR/DD programs include a variety of programs for persons of all ages with mental retardation and developmental disabilities, although the vast majority of beneficiaries are adults. Agency activities include operating and/or funding residential facilities and providing community services. An estimated $557 million in federal funds and $821 million in state funds (including Medicaid) were spent by these programs on children in 1992. State mental health and substance abuse service programs serve persons of all ages. They usually include special programs for adolescents with serious mental illness. Services include inpatient, residential, outpatient, and emergency services; these agencies often run state psychiatric hospitals. In 1990, 80 percent of funding was from the state, with an additional 9 percent from federal Medicaid funds. An estimated 10 percent of total state mental health agency funds, or $1.2 billion (including Medicaid), was spent on services for children and adolescents. Table 2.5 lists unduplicated (non-Medicaid) funding separately for these programs.[26]

• Head Start provides comprehensive developmental services for low-income preschool-aged children. At least 10 percent of each program's enrollment slots must be available to children with disabilities. Of the 713,903 children enrolled in Head Start in 1993, over 13 percent (or 94,000 children) had a disability. The Head Start Bureau estimates that *additional* services for children with disabilities account for only 3.3 percent of total Head Start expenditures, or approximately $92 million in federal funds and $23 million in state funds in 1993.

Total Government Expenditures

To enhance our understanding of the relative importance of each program to the whole system, we estimate total expenditures for the major government programs serving children with disabilities. As we do not include some smaller programs serving this population, this estimate understates *all* government expenditures for children with disabilities. As much as possible, these figures represent unduplicated expenditures to avoid overestimating spending. Medicaid dollars pay for services provided through many different programs, including several programs covered in Table 2.5. In the table, however, all Medicaid dollars are reported in the row devoted to Medicaid and expenditures for other programs reflect funding from sources *other than* Medicaid.[27]

We estimate total annual expenditures by major government programs serving children with disabilities at $44.3 billion in 1993: $10.6 billion by the federal government and $33.7 billion by state and local governments. State and local governments are spending more than three times what federal programs are spending. Total government spending at all levels on children with disabilities is almost ten times the value of cash benefits provided by the SSI program to eligible children.

Looking at the system as a whole, by far the largest share of expenditures is for education and related services: $31.6 billion. Medical or health services are the second largest type of benefit, ranging from $6.3 to $7.9 billion.[28] The third largest benefit type is cash, through SSI, at $4.3 billion, which parents may choose to spend on education or medical services. Unlike most of the health and cash benefits, eligibility for education benefits is not based on family income.

Almost two-thirds of federal spending is from two programs: SSI and Medicaid. Much of the remaining third is spending for special education programs. The vast majority of state and local spending (86 percent) is for special education programs. Remaining state spending is mostly through Medicaid, either directly for the state share of basic health services or as a funding stream for other programs. Therefore, in terms of overall spending by programs for children with disabilities, special education is first, Medicaid second, and SSI is third. The remaining programs are small in comparison to these, although they fill important gaps.

These expenditures are not "incremental" expenditures, those associated only with the child's disability. For example, special education expenditures are not measured over and above public education system costs for children without disabilities. Similarly, Medicaid costs for these children are not limited to those related to disabilities alone.[29]

Therefore, for most of these programs, expenditure levels should not be interpreted as the amount that would be "saved" by the government if that program no longer existed or stopped serving children with disabilities. If these program expenditures were not made, some or all of these expenditures would shift to other government programs.

For example, some of the expenditures made by special education programs would be paid for by general public school funds. Many children with disabilities are eligible for Medicaid because they receive SSI benefits, but they would be eligible for Medicaid based on other factors. Similarly, if children were to no longer receive SSI cash payments, many would qualify for AFDC benefits.

Also, aggregate spending and participation in public programs for children with disabilities masks large variation within programs across children, in terms of needs and expenditures per child. Table 2.6 reports two examples, from Medicaid and Special Education, of variation in costs across children receiving services. For Medicaid, we can see that children receiving in-patient psychiatric services or services from intermediate care facilities for mentally retarded per-

Table 2.6 EXAMPLES OF VARIATION IN SPENDING PER CHILD WITHIN PUBLIC PROGRAMS SERVING CHILDREN WITH DISABILITIES

Medicaid
Average Annual Per Child Expenditures
by Service Receipt, 1993

All Services for Blind and Disabled Children	$7,352
Inpatient Psychiatric Services	$20,319
Intermediate Care Facilities for Mental Retardation Services	$54,384

Special Education
Per Pupil Expenditures by Major Program Type and Disability,
School Year 1985–86 (in Current Year Dollars)

For children with Autism:	
Preschool	$6,265
Self-contained	$7,582
Resource room	NA
Resource, self-contained, home/hospital, and residential	$17,236
For children with Specific Learning Disabilities:	
Preschool	$3,708
Self-contained	$3,083
Resource room	$1,643
Resource, self-contained, home/hospital, and residential	$2,058

Sources: Medicaid—Urban Institute calculations from HCFA forms 2082 and 64. Special Education—Stephen Chaikind, Louis C. Danielson, and Marsha L. Brauen, "What Do We Know About the Costs of Special Education? A Selected Review," *The Journal of Special Education*, Vol. 26, No. 4, 1993, drawing on data reported in Mary T. Moore, E. William Strang, Myron Schwartz, and Mark Braddock, *Patterns in Special Education Service Delivery and Cost* (U.S. Department of Education Contract No. 300-84-0257), Decision Resources Corporation, Washington, D.C., December 1988.

sons (ICF/MR) have much higher annual costs on average than the expenditures per blind or disabled child over all service types. For special education, costs differ by program type as well as by disability. Expenditures per pupil in any given program type are higher for children with autism than for those with a specific learning disability. These differences reflect variation in the severity of disability by condition, as well as variation in costs associated with each program type.

From reviewing the major programs serving children with disabilities and estimated total expenditures made by these programs, we can develop some ideas about the function of the system's parts and the relative size of these parts across program, level of government, and type of benefit. We still lack important information on how the parts fit together. For example, we do not have the necessary information to develop an unduplicated count of the total number of children receiving services from this system. Because the programs provide different services, many children receive assistance from more than one program. Therefore, totaling the number of children served by each program would overestimate the number of children with disabilities served. Not knowing how many children are benefiting from multiple programs limits our ability to assess the strengths and weaknesses of the system.

Of course, not all children with disabilities need the same mix of services. Better understanding of the needs of these children and their families, coupled with information about services they are receiving, is important. This is especially true of programs that are primarily administered at the local level and for which communities have a great deal of discretion and autonomy in determining what services are provided and how. For example, we know very little about the numbers and types of children receiving various combinations of specific services through their special education programs. In addition, information on the social, demographic, and economic characteristics of children and families served are for the most part unavailable, making it difficult to assess service distribution within the eligible population. This type of information could help us evaluate the extent to which this system of programs is working and how it might be improved.

Private Expenditures

Although the focus of this study is on government programs, public expenditures by these programs represent only that portion of the total costs borne by taxpayers in general. Of great importance are the many direct and indirect "private" costs incurred by families. Although family costs have been frequently overlooked in policy discussions, private/family costs and public costs are not independent of one another.[30] A family who prefers to care for a child at home, but cannot afford to do so without some type of financial subsidy, may resort to placing their child in an institution, at a much higher public cost (compared to a small subsidy). These types of interactions mean that some measures that appear to cut costs may simply result in cost shifting. Understanding public and private costs of caring for children with disabilities, and how these costs are distributed, would help inform important choices when designing and administering programs: e.g., subsidies, tax deductions, or credits to assist families as they care for children with disabilities.

The direct private costs families face are for items and services as varied as those provided by public programs. The most recognized direct private cost is for medical expenses paid out-of-pocket. Indeed, studies indicate that families of children with disabilities do bear higher medical expenses than other families. However, there are many other direct expenses families face including special food, clothing, and assistive equipment, car and home modifications, specialized child care or respite care, and individual or family counseling. In addition to these costs, the indirect or opportunity costs of forgone income due to time spent caring for children with disabilities needs to be considered. There are few empirical estimates of the full costs of caring for chronically ill and disabled children and those studies that exist are limited, often considering only a specific type of disability. A review of the studies on medical and non-medical private costs of caring for children with disabilities is included in Appendix B.

While evidence regarding the private family costs associated with raising a child with a disability is limited, it does indicate that these costs are high and vary across many dimensions, including type of disability, family, and community, as well as over time for the same family. Costs to families are not only economic, but also psychosocial. For example, two families with similar economic circumstances may differ greatly in their ability to care for a child with a disability. And, of course, the availability of community-level support services and public programs may affect how well families are able to care for a child with a disability. Easing the costs to such families is, at least in part, a motivating factor in creating public programs.

CONCLUSIONS

Clearly the system of programs serving children with disabilities and their families is large and complex. If policymakers and researchers often lack a comprehensive overview of the system, imagine how much more confusing the system may be to families needing access to some of these programs.

Based on this overview, it is now possible to make some definitive statements about the relationship among these programs. These programs struggle with difficult issues of definition and measurement and are not always consistent in the ways they determine eligibility. They provide assistance in a society that includes as many as 4.5 million disabled children, more than 20 percent of whom are estimated to be severely disabled. Many additional children are in need of various forms of mental health services. Indeed, the nation's school systems are providing special education and related services to more than 5 million children annually. Expenditures of $44.3 billion in 1993 were dominated by spending of state and local governments, primarily for education and related services. Of next order of importance were health expenditures and related programs which themselves were often financed under Medicaid at both the federal and state and local levels. Unlike many health benefits and almost all cash benefits, education benefits are not based on financial need.

It is our hope that this comprehensive overview will help citizens and policymakers to understand better how the system is evolving and to consider more carefully where they would like it to head. To make informed choices for the future, however, also requires a consideration of principles and reasonable tradeoffs among them. It is to that issue that we next turn.

Notes

1. Indeed, one source reports 43 different definitions of disability among federal disability programs and hundreds more among state and local programs. See Michele Adler, "Programmatic Definitions of Disability: Policy Implications," *1991 Proceedings of the Government Statistics Section, American Statistical Association*, Alexandria, Virginia, 1991.

2. This discussion benefitted especially from Ellen C. Perrin, Paul Newacheck, Barry Pless, et al., "Issues Involved in the Definition and Classification of Chronic Health Conditions," *Pediatrics*, Vol. 91, No. 4, April 1993.

3. Appendix A provides a detailed review of the major data sources used to study children with disabilities.

4. V. Benson and M.A. Marano, *Current Estimates from the National Health Interview Survey, 1993*, National Center for Health Statistics, Vital Health Statistics, Series 10, No. 190, December 1994.

5. See Saad Z. Nagi, "Disability Concepts Revisited: Implications for Prevention," pp. 309–327 in Andrew M. Pope and Alvin R. Tarlow (eds.), *Disability in America: Towards a National Agenda for Prevention*, National Academy Press, Washington, D.C., 1991.

6. A second widely cited framework is the International Classification of Impairments, Disabilities, and Handicaps (ICIDH). The ICIDH is a trial supplement to the World Health Organization's (WHO) International Classification of Diseases. For a review of ICIDH see World Health Organization, *International Classification of Impairments, Disabilities, and Handicaps: A manual of classification relating to the consequences of disease*, WHO, Geneva, Switzerland, 1980.

7. Just as impairments do not necessarily result in a functional limitation, impairments and functional limitations do not necessarily cause disabilities. Furthermore, depending on the individual, similar impairments and functional limitations may lead to very different types of disabilities.

8. Nagi, "Disability Concepts Revisited," 1991.

9. Ibid.

10. This section and the one that follows, "Measuring Needs," are adapted from a text originally authored by Rune J. Simeonsson of the University of North Carolina at Chapel Hill.

10. E. Sinclair, S.R. Forness, and J. Alexson, *The Journal of Special Education*, 19(3), 1985, pp. 333–344.

12. B.L. Mallory and G.M. Kerns, "Consequences of Categorical Labeling of Preschool Children," *TECSE*, 8(3), 1988, pp. 39–50.

13. C. Wolman, M.L. Thurlow, and R.H. Bruininks, "Stability of Categorical Designations for Special Education Students: A Longitudinal Study," *The Journal of Special Education*, 23(2), 1989, pp. 213–222.

14. B.J. Smith and J.A. Schakel, "Noncategorical Identification of Preschool Handicapped Children: Policy Issues and Options," *Journal of the Division for Early Childhood*, 11(10), 1986, pp. 78–86; R.J. Simeonsson, and D.B. Bailey, "Essential Elements of the Assessment Process," in T.D. Wachs and R. Sheehan (eds.), *Assessment of Young Developmentally Disabled Children*, New York: Plenum Press, 1988, pp. 25–42; R.E. Stein, and D.J. Jessop, "What Diagnosis Does Not Tell: The Case for a Noncategorical Approach to Chronic Illness in Childhood," *Social Science in Medicine*, 29(6), 1989, pp. 769–778.

15. M.C. Reynolds, A.G. Zetlin, and M.C. Wang, "20/20 Analysis: Taking a Close Look at the Margins," *Exceptional Children*, 59(4), 1993, pp. 294–300.

16. Representative measures for adults include the Functional Independence Measure-FIM and the Barthel ADL Index and the WeeFim and the ABILITIES Index for children. See C. Collin, D.T. Wade, S. Davies, and V. Horne, "The Barthel ADL Index: A Reliability Study," *International Disabilities Studies*, 10, 1988, pp. 61–63 and R.J. Simeonsson, D.B. Bailey, T. Smith, and V. Buysse, "Young Children with Disabilities: Functional Assessment by Teachers," *Journal of Developmental and Physical Disabilities* 7(4), 1995, pp. 267–284.

17. R.J.V. Montgomery, D.E. Stull, and E.F. Borgatta, "Measurement and the Analysis of Burden," *Research on Aging*, 7(1), 1985, pp. 137–152.

18. M.I. Benedict, L.M. Wulff, and R.B. White, "Current Parental Stress in Maltreating and Nonmaltreating Families of Children with Multiple Disabilities," *Child Abuse and Neglect*, Vol. 16, No. 2, 1992, pp. 155–163 and D.A. Whyte, "The Family Nursing Approach to the Care of a Child with a Chronic Illness," *Journal of Advanced Nursing*, 17(3), 1992, pp. 317–327.

19. E. Bonwich and J.C. Reid, "Medical Rehabilitation: Issues in Assessment of Functional Change," *Evaluation Practice*, Vol. 12, No. 3, 1991, pp. 205–215.

20. P. Jacobs and S. McDermott, "Family Caregiver Costs of Chronically Ill and Handicapped Children: Method and Literature Review," *Public Health Reports*, Vol. 104, No. 2, 1989, pp. 158–163; and B. Leonard, J.D. Brust, and J.J. Sapienza, "Financial and Time Costs to Parents of Severely Disabled Children," *Public Health Reports*, Vol. 107, No. 3, 1992, pp. 302–312; and G. Barabas, W. Matthews, and P. Zumoff, "Careload for Children and Young Adults with Severe Cerebral Palsy," *Developmental Medicine and Child Neurology*, 34, 1992, pp. 979–984.

21. SIPP is based on a nationally-representative sample of households from the civilian non-institutional population and disability-related questions vary according to the age of the child. For a more detailed discussion of the child disability questions in SIPP, see Appendix A, Sources of National Data on Children with Disabilities.

22. See, for example, Daniel P. Hallahan, "Some Thoughts on Why the Prevalence of Learning Disabilities Has Increased," *Journal of Learning Disabilities*, Vol. 25, No. 8, October 1992.

23. The National Institute of Mental Health has been planning a child psychiatric program to obtain comprehensive information on the prevalence of mental disorders among children and youth and on their use of mental health services. This effort is described in more detail in Center for Mental Health Services, *Mental Health, United States, 1994*, R.W. Manderscheid and M.A. Sonnenschein (eds.), DHHS Pub. No. (SMA) 94-3000, Washington, D.C., 1994.

24. U.S. Congress, Office of Technology Assessment, *Children's Mental Health: Problems and Services—A Background Paper*, OTA-BP-H-33, U.S. Government Printing Office, Washington, D.C., December 1986.

25. The counts of children served and total expenditures for Medicaid are likely underestimates because these numbers only include children eligible for Medicaid through SSI or who are receiving long-term care services through Medicaid. Other children with disabilities who are not eligible for SSI but are receiving Medicaid services are not included in these estimates. See the section on Medicaid in Chapter 4 of Part II for additional discussion of this potential underestimate.

26. In the table, we attempt to provide an unduplicated estimate of total spending. Therefore, expenditures reported for state MR/DD programs and state mental health programs do not reflect their total budgets, but rather expenditures less Medicaid funding.

27. For some programs we had to make assumptions in order to separate out funding sources, federal versus state expenditures, or expenditures on adults versus children.

28. If only Medicaid and Title V, Children with Special Health Care Needs are included the figure is $6.3 billion. Including MR/DD and mental health programs, which include many non-medical support services as well as direct health services, raises the total to $7.9 billion.

29. The only exception to this is for Head Start, where we include only the additional expenditures made on special services for these children.

30. Other private-sector expenditures made on behalf of children with disabilities include those made by private foundations and other charitable organizations. Unfortunately, an examination of these non-family private costs is beyond the scope of this study.

References for Table 2.5

Braddock, David, Richard Hemp, Lynn Bachelder, and Glenn Fujiura, *The State of the States in Developmental Disabilities*, Institute on Disability and Human Development, The University of Illinois at Chicago, October 1994.

Center for Mental Health Services and the National Institute of Mental Health, *Mental Health, United States, 1992*, R.W. Manderscheid and M.A. Sonnenchien (eds.), DHHS Pub. No. (SMA) 92-1942, Washington, D.C., 1992.

Hoagwood, Kimberly and Agnes Rupp, "Mental Health Service Needs, Use, and Costs for Children and Adolescents with Mental Disorders and their Families: Preliminary Evidence" in Center for Mental Health Services, *Mental Health, United States, 1994*, R.W. Manderscheid and M.A. Sonnenchien (eds.), DHHS Pub. No. (SMA) 94-3000, Washington, D.C., 1994.

National Association of State Mental Health Program Directors Research Institute, *Funding Sources and Expenditures of State Mental Health Agencies: Revenue/Expenditure Study Results Fiscal Year 1990*, Alexandria, VA, 1993.

U.S. Department of Education, *To Assure the Free Appropriate Public Education of All Children With Disabilities: Sixteenth Annual Report to Congress on the Implementation of the Individuals with Disabilities Education Act, Report to Congress on Fiscal Year 1991: Maternal and Child Health Activities and Health Status*, Rockville, MD, January 1995.

U.S. Social Security Administration, *Annual Statistical Supplement to the Social Security Bulletin*, Washington, D.C., 1994.

Chapter Three

APPLYING PRINCIPLES TO COMPLEX PROGRAM CHOICES

Legislation affecting Americans with disabilities articulates many noble and worthy goals. The Americans with Disabilities Act (ADA) of 1990 declares that "the Nation's proper goals regarding individuals with disabilities are to assure equality of opportunity, full participation, independent living, and economic self-sufficiency for such individuals." Similarly, the Rehabilitation Act of 1973 was designed to "empower individuals with disabilities to maximize employment, economic self-sufficiency, independence, and inclusion and integration into society."

For children with disabilities, the declared goals are no less ambitious. The Individual with Disabilities Education Act (IDEA) intends "to assure that all children with disabilities have available to them . . . a free appropriate public education which emphasizes special education and related services designed to meet their unique needs, to assure that the rights of children with disabilities and their parents or guardians are protected, to assist states and localities to provide for the education of all children with disabilities, and to assess and assure the effectiveness of efforts to educate children with disabilities."

As these legislative goals illustrate, the U.S. aspires to provide full opportunities for independence, productivity, and social integration of persons with disabilities. Despite the progress that has been made thus far, most observers agree that there is still a long way to go before the ideals embedded in the ADA and IDEA are realized.

There are many reasons why, as a society, we have not yet achieved equal opportunity, maximum employment or independence, or a free "appropriate" education for all persons with disabilities. One is the recency of some legislative efforts, such as the ADA, which was widely hailed as a landmark piece of legislation. A second is that society's efforts to remove barriers to participation and inclusion (barriers which may be physical, legal, or attitudinal), to empower people

*Americans aspire to provide full
opportunities for independence,
productivity, and social integration of
persons with disabilities.*

with disabilities, and to provide them with benefits and services, compete among themselves and with other societal goals that require scarce resources.

Scarcity of resources inevitably implies that choices must be made involving trade-offs among different goals. Total expenditures on government programs for children with disabilities depend partly upon the overall level of available public resources and partly upon other demands for these resources, such as for higher education, justice, national defense, and interest on the debt. While political constraints sometimes dictate that choices on allocating scarce resources be made implicitly, logic argues that society as a whole may gain if it pays explicit attention to deciding how each dollar can be spent best. Even if some optimal level of total spending on programs for children with disabilities could be known and agreed upon by society, choices still would be required. Existing public resources are almost inevitably inadequate to meet all needs and demands for education, health services, cash assistance, or other government services. Further, progress toward attaining goals can always be dampened or enhanced depending upon how well and efficiently resources are allocated and used.

This chapter provides an integrated approach or framework for examining the choices that must be made as this broad system of programs continues to evolve. It offers a systematic means to relate many of the competing goals that face society in allocating program expenditures for children with disabilities.

*Broader programmatic choices being made
by society should be viewed as a whole,
not as disconnected parts.*

One reason an integrated framework is timely is that in recent years there has been increased budgetary scrutiny of many public programs, including those for children with disabilities. This need not be a threatening prospect. When there is a common focus on trying to meet goals more effectively, the tension between goals and budgets can be a healthy one. Even in a growing economy that makes available increased resources to the public sector, society and policymakers must still choose how to govern that growth in a reasonable and considered manner.

A strong warning is required: using a systematic and comprehensive framework for dealing with very complex choices is by no means an easy task. But it is an unavoidable one. Without such an approach, programs serving children with disabilities are unlikely to evolve in ways that allocate money to where it can be spent most effectively or where needs are greatest. Necessary program refinements may go unrecognized or ignored. Allocation of program resources may become unrelated to actual, documented, needs. Some children with significant needs may receive a smaller share of resources than appropriate, while in other cases program investments may not produce expected outcomes, such as the enhanced development of the child. Some needs of children may not be addressed or identified, while the services provided may not always be those that are most beneficial. Although examining choices in a systematic manner does not insure that these problems will be resolved, it does "frame" issues so that they can be treated more comprehensively, consistently, and, hopefully, in a way that will achieve greater benefit for each dollar spent.

Without a systematic and comprehensive approach, children with significant needs may receive a smaller share of resources than appropriate, while in other cases program investments may not produce expected outcomes.

Making choices systematically and through a common framework may also help achieve greater consensus on priorities. During periods of budget scrutiny, there is a danger that positions will become polarized. As noted by Mashaw, real needs may not be met when there are "public perceptions of abuse," while "those active in disability advocacy can be pushed into rigid defensive postures that transform needed programmatic adjustments into the political equivalent of trench warfare."[1] When such conflicts dominate the discussion, it is often difficult to set priorities according to any standard. In theory, a better route to handle the tension is for citizens and their government, having established a general set of common goals and objectives, to determine priorities according to principles and practical considerations of what can be administered, and then to establish clear steps to carry out those priorities. Regardless of the total level of resources available to serve and support children with disabilities, society should face dilemmas and constraints honestly and consider what types of efforts are likely to be most beneficial at that level or any other level that might be attained.

PRINCIPLES

Here we propose a set of principles or guidelines which may help determine priorities and channel resources in disability programs. This framework is not intended to prescribe societal choices as to what dollars should be spent on which programs. It does, however, provide a basis for thinking systematically about the relationship between general goals and available resources. While our emphasis is on programs for children with disabilities and their families, many implications extend to other government programs.

The principles set out here reflect common-sense notions of promoting fairness, effectiveness, and individual development.

The principles we set out here are found in one form or another in discussions of public policy, public finance, social welfare policy, and economics. They reflect commonly accepted notions of promoting fairness, effectiveness, and individual development. The principles, as applied to government benefits, are as follows:

- program benefits should relate to needs;
- people with equal needs and equal levels of resources should receive equal treatment;
- programs should deliver services and benefits in ways that develop individual and family capabilities and enhance self-sufficiency;
- programs should operate effectively and efficiently; and
- program benefits should reflect levels of individual contributions, in cases where individuals can and do make direct contributions.

Each of these principles is discussed in more detail below.

RELATING BENEFITS TO NEEDS (PROGRESSIVITY)

Addressing needs is the underlying rationale for most publicly-funded social programs. While individual motivations and philosophies for social programs may be multiple—a sense of moral obligation, goodwill, social contract, or, simply, mutual concern—government involvement is usually a consequence of some members of society having needs that are not being effectively met elsewhere. Government programs, of course, also involve pooling societal resources. Clearly these resources should be directed toward actual, documented, needs. In the case of children with disabilities, this principle often suggests that public resources (benefits less taxes) be targeted toward those more in need (or with fewer means), also known as progressivity.[2]

If individuals could be ranked on their differing abilities and advantages, the progressivity principle argues that those at the top of the scale would transfer the most assistance and those at the bottom would receive the greatest transfers.

The extent of progressivity (indeed, the degree to which this principle is accepted) is still a societal choice. If individuals could be ranked on their differing abilities and advantages (or disabilities and disadvantages), the progressivity principle argues that on net those at the top of the scale would transfer the most assistance and those at the bottom would receive the greatest transfers. The principle, by itself, does not state how extensive the net transfers should be, only that the direction is increasingly from the well-off to the less well-off.[3]

There are important issues surrounding which documented needs of which individuals should be met when resources are limited. For instance, in some cases priorities are given to persons with the most severe disabilities—a position generally defended on grounds that they have the greatest need for assistance. It should be noted, however, that there is not perfect correspondence between need for assistance and severity of disability. Furthermore, levels of need may not correspond either to the ability of resources to make a difference or to the ultimate payoff from an investment of public resources.

Assuring Fairness and Equity (Equal Treatment of Equals)

A second principle, closely related to the first, is among the most universally accepted of all principles. An established program should serve equally two persons in equal circumstances (usually defined by either or both needs and means—disabilities and abilities, including

---

The concept of "equal treatment of equals" is at the heart of many American ideals.

---

income). This concept of "equal treatment of equals" is at the heart of many American ideals, and is found in our system of jurisprudence and the U.S. Constitution in standards such as "equal justice." Its antecedents are much older: according to Aristotle, justice involves treating equals equally (this principle) and unequals unequally proportionate to their differences (the principle of progressivity enunciated above). In the context of this study, equal treatment of equals generally means that those children with disabilities who have similar needs and equally scarce resources should be treated equally. Like the other principles examined here, putting into practice equal treatment of equals may be difficult. It requires valid and reliable measures of the existence and severity of a disability, the needs of the individual, and family-level resources available to meet the needs.

Government programs should be aimed at both the long-term and short-term well-being of society. In general, investment is future-oriented and by its very nature implies some sacrifice of consumption today to promote greater well-being tomorrow. In the context of this

---

Relating services to a plan for the individual is a method of investment deeply imbedded in federal law, for example, in individualized written rehabilitation plans in vocational education, and in individualized education plans in special education.

---

study, the principle implies that disability programs should be oriented as a whole toward assisting children with disabilities and their families to become more self-sufficient. Under this principle, a program's benefits and services should not only supplement, but complement, a child and family's inherent strengths and abilities. Programs ideally should be flexible enough to accommodate the many varied strengths of children and their families and assist them in developing their natural and inherent potential to help themselves. Relating services to a plan for the individual is a method of investment deeply imbedded in federal law, for example, in individualized written rehabilitation plans in vocational education, and in individualized education plans and individualized transition plans in special education. The goals of economic self-sufficiency and independence—incorporated into the language of many legislative enactments such as the Americans with Disabilities Act (ADA) and the Rehabilitation Act of 1973—are also specific reflections of this broader principle.

In theory, any government program should seek to maximize the well-being of society for each dollar spent. Given a level of resources within a particular disability program, each program dollar spent should make the greatest improvement possible in the quality of life of per-

> *A more efficient program may be able to
> serve more children or serve the same
> number of children better than a
> comparable but less efficient program.*

sons assisted. All other things equal, a more efficient program may be able to serve more children or serve the same number of children better than a comparable but less efficient program. Note that considerations of equity and efficiency often go hand in hand. For example, efforts to educate children with disabilities alongside other children are likely to be motivated both by a sense of fairness and some notion that it will be more effective or efficient in educating them.

RESPECTING INDIVIDUAL EQUITY (RELATING BENEFITS TO
INDIVIDUAL CONTRIBUTIONS)

The principle of individual equity is applied primarily to programs in which individuals make a direct contribution. In the broadest sense, the principle recognizes the importance of "quid pro quo" or "getting what you pay for." Retirement and disability programs for adults, such as Social Security Old Age and Disability Insurance (OASDI), for example, relate benefits to contributions.[4] Although individual contributions are only occasionally made directly to disability programs for children, the principle is listed here primarily because programs for children are sometimes contrasted with programs for adults. When adults receive higher payments than children with equal or greater needs, these differences probably rely substantially upon an appeal to this principle. Adults who have contributed to a program, for instance, might be deemed as worthy of having their wages replaced at the time of disability even though these cash benefits might be much higher than those offered to families of children with disabilities.[5] Although this principle is less applicable to programs for children by themselves, relating benefits to contributions often conflicts with the earlier principle of relating benefits to needs, and balance must be sought.

Setting Boundaries

Although these guidelines or principles follow commonly accepted notions of fairness, efficiency, and individual development, they are difficult to put into practice. Sometimes they conflict with each other and require judgment as to their relative importance. Sometimes the more complete fulfillment of one principle means a less complete fulfillment of another. Often, the conflict is determining the net gain within a single principle: for example, greater individual discretion may make a program more efficient in accommodating resources to individual needs, but less efficient in minimizing administrative costs.

Sometimes the principles conflict with each other and require judgment as to their relative importance. Still, they can be used to frame or bound a reasonable set of policy alternatives.

So why go through all this trouble if compromises are required in any case? The power of principles and guidelines is that they can be used to frame or bound a reasonable set of policy alternatives. They compel decision-makers to think concretely in terms of the gains and losses inherent in different resource allocation decisions. Among other elements of rigor, they demand attention to how each dollar is spent, regardless of whether the total is viewed as too low, just adequate, or too high.

The violation of any one principle can be justified only if an action furthers some other principle, and even then the balance must be examined critically. For instance, suppose a program provides different levels of assistance to families in equal need and with equally few family resources. Such inequities could be justified mainly if there were identifiable efficiency gains, in particular, from experimentation or from taking advantage of different capabilities among jurisdictions. But if the inequities are arbitrary and there is little or no reason to expect gains in efficiency, then the design of the program does not fit within the boundaries established by the principles. Over the past hundred years, this particular tension between equity and efficiency has played itself out in the cycling of program control to and from the federal level (where equity may be fulfilled) and the state and local levels (where efficiency may be higher). A framework of principles forces one to think in such a rigorous and consistent way; it does not produce any absolute answers. Society must still make choices.

In the remainder of this chapter we apply these principles to some of the difficult choices confronting programs for children with disabilities. We point out the trade-offs between principles inherent in designing and implementing programs to reach society's goals for these children and their families. The examples are meant to make concrete the exercise of applying this framework to making policy decisions in this area, although it is not our task to make final choices. Hopefully, these examples will help policymakers to continue applying this framework to questions and issues not considered here.

The range of issues that can be presented in any one study is necessarily limited. Among the issues *not* explored in depth here, although the principles clearly apply, is how children with disabilities and their families as a group should fare in the allocation of government resources relative to other worthy societal needs, including but not limited to all disability-related programs.[6]

Among the difficult issues we examine here, and which are informed by these principles, are:

- Who should be served? Should a program lean toward errors of exclusion of some who are in need or inclusion of some who are not in need? Should programs be targeted or universal in nature? Can benefits be gradated according to need?
- What types of benefits should be provided? Should they aim at support or investment in the individual? Which is preferable: cash or in-kind benefits?
- What are some of the incentives that can affect the ability of programs to meet various goals fairly and efficiently?

This list is not comprehensive and the issues of eligibility and types of benefits are often not separable. Nonetheless, it does contain issues that are regularly discussed, although seldom systematically addressed, by those attempting to design and improve programs for children with disabilities.

WHO BENEFITS

Perhaps the first question addressed in designing programs for children with disabilities is, "Who is to be served?" Almost all social programs must define their beneficiaries, and the jump from theory to practice is never easy. Defining the intended beneficiaries in programs for children with disabilities is complicated by particularly difficult measurement problems. Many of these problems were discussed in Chapter 2 and are illustrated by the wide variation in estimates of the number of children with disabilities. Nonetheless, definition of eligibles is crucial to put many principles into practice—for example, to treat equals equally requires that they be equally eligible for program participation.

Errors of Inclusion or Exclusion

All programs that have disability as part of their eligibility criteria face these difficult measurement problems. It is not surprising, therefore, that there is variation across programs and over time in disability determinations. Even society's concept of disability has evolved as its knowledge base and technological capabilities have grown. The difficulty of measurement, however, adds to the likelihood of program error. Society often responds to these errors by trying to develop a better knowledge base or by shifting its definition of eligibility in ways that could both include new recipients or activities and exclude old ones.

Society's concept of disability has evolved as its knowledge base and technological capabilities have grown.

In defining program eligibility, there are two kinds of potential error: providing benefits to some children who are not technically eligible for those benefits (errors of inclusion) and denying benefits to some children who really should receive benefits (errors of exclusion). These errors apply to both the basic eligibility criteria governing a program (e.g., what types of disabilities and other criteria qualify a child for benefits or services) and the manner in which these criteria are implemented or operationalized (e.g., how disability is measured).

Government officials in charge of administering programs sometimes argue that we should have a "zero tolerance" for fraud and abuse. While no one is in favor of expending resources on individuals who are ineligible for a program, in practice the cost of such a policy includes a greater number of exclusion errors—some children who are eligible for benefits will not receive them. Exactly the opposite problem, of course, is created by attempting zero error on the inclusion side.

In practice the cost of a policy of zero tolerance for fraud includes a greater number of exclusion errors. Exactly the opposite problem, of course, is created by attempting zero error on the inclusion side.

Either type of error violates the principle of fairness or equal treatment of equals. Two individuals who are "equally" eligible for the program are not treated equally if one receives the benefit and the other does not. Like so many of the dilemmas we examine, there are no easy answers. A balance between both types of errors must eventually be made. But there are ways in which gradual overall improvement can be attained.

More accurate measurement of disability and the accompanying needs of the family uniquely serves to reduce both types of error at the same time. Research into better or more easily implemented measures can potentially be used to target resources more fairly and efficiently. Regular reviews of disability determination also help ensure over time that initial errors in eligibility determination are corrected. Audit functions within disability programs might be converted into better statistical bases for measuring—not just auditing—how accurately a program is targeting its population.

A related approach is to consider carefully and rigorously the types of errors created by different types of criteria. For example, using a set of medical conditions as eligibility criteria may be simpler and less subjective than functional limitation determinations, thus limiting some types of inclusion errors and creating greater administrative certainty.[7] However, given variation in severity of disability within groups of children with the same condition, lists of diagnoses may not as easily allow targeting of benefits to the most severely disabled children as functional limitation criteria. For example, the Individual Functional Assessment used in the SSI program involves complex criteria for weighing a child's functional abilities. Using these criteria

> *The Individual Functional Assessment in SSI may produce more inclusion errors than lists of medical conditions. But relying on these lists may end up excluding children with great needs.*

may produce more inclusion errors than lists of medical conditions. But relying on these lists may end up excluding children with great needs who do not meet one of the listings.

Targeted versus Universal Programs

Program services and benefits delivered to children with disabilities and their families are usually designed to meet specific types of needs (be they educational, medical, economic, or psychological). Since scarce resources almost inevitably mean that public programs will use cut-offs, programs often will restrict benefits to a limited set of eligible persons, as defined by the greatest or most identifiable needs. As the principle of progressivity affirms, this is one reason why there are such programs in the first place.

However, there is a tension between how to provide benefits. One option for programs is that they serve *all* children with disabilities (or certain types of disabilities), irrespective of any other individual or family-level characteristics. Special education is one example of a more "universal" program.[8]

A second approach is to target (or limit) program benefits to specific subgroups of children with disabilities defined by whether a family is able to meet a child's needs with its own resources, typically mean-

> *Special education is one example of a more "universal" program. SSI and Medicaid, on the other hand, target program benefits to those children whose families' economic circumstances are limited.*

ing programs serve poor or near-poor families only (SSI and Medicaid are examples) or by some dimension of disability, for example severity or duration (SSI and workers' compensation are examples). Because targeting limits overall program costs, it allows a greater share of resources to be devoted to the targeted population and, in principle, to those with the greatest needs. This approach attempts to enhance progressivity within the program itself, whereas a more universal program can achieve similar progressivity only by imposing efficiency costs in terms of higher taxation of the non-eligible population.

At one level, both universal and targeted approaches attempt to apply an "equal treatment of equals" standard *among* program eligibles. In the first case "equality" is a function of a child's disability only, while in the second case, equality is measured in terms both of family income and the child's disability. The issue, however, is much more complex. If a family member has a moderate or severe disability, and receives no adjustment in either benefits or taxes, then society effectively grants that family equal treatment to another family in the same circumstances (e.g., income) *other than* the disability. Few, however, would believe these families to be in equal circumstances *overall*.[9] Restricting all adjustments for the costs of disabilities to only low-income families, therefore, could be viewed as a violation of the principle of "equal treatment of equals" by ignoring the impact of the disability on defining who are equals.

Targeting can also have some severe side effects. As we discuss later, it can create some perverse incentives to avoid work, limit savings, or other activities that may make the family ineligible for benefits. That is, targeting involves high tax rates on the income of potentially eligible families. Targeting often involves higher administrative expenses per person served (e.g., to document or verify initial eligibility criteria, determine continued program eligibility, etc.), which decreases efficiency.

Because targeting limits overall program costs, it does allow a greater share of resources to be devoted to the targeted population and, in principle, to the greatest needs. It can have some severe side effects, however.

Targeting puts pressure on the measures used to differentiate among individuals. Income, for instance, is often a poor measure of need or potential economic resources, especially when family members are capable of work. Compared to some other criteria, however, income is relatively easy to measure. Translating concepts used for targeting, such as "severely disabled," into eligibility criteria is more difficult. When measuring need, it is also difficult to take into account factors that may affect a family's ability to care for a child, such as a family's emotional and psychological strengths and broader family and community support systems.

Often policymakers will move even further away from universal programs by setting up queues. Initial eligibility criteria may be universal or targeted by income levels, but, to further reduce costs, there is a restriction on the number who will be served, often determined on a first-come, first-served, basis. Some educational programs, such as Head Start, operate in this manner. Unfortunately, as a compromise, this type of approach tends especially to violate the principle of equal treatment of equals and is often less progressive than a program which is more narrowly targeted. The approach does limit costs, if in an arbitrary manner.

One long-recognized area of concern that stems from targeting is the potentially detrimental effects of "labeling" or categorizing children, a process that arises in a variety of contexts, including attempts to target benefits. As Nicholas Hobbs and his colleagues observed twenty years ago:

> Children who are categorized and labeled as different may be permanently stigmatized, rejected by adults and other children, and excluded from opportunities essential for their full and healthy development. Yet categorization is necessary to open doors to opportunity: to get help for a child, to write legislation, to appropriate funds, to design service programs, to evaluate outcomes, to conduct research, even to communicate about the problems of an exceptional child.[10]

While evidence is unclear as to whether labeling by programs has detrimental effects beyond "societal" labeling that occurs in its absence, program implementation can still lead to negative effects. Thus, the label of having a learning disability may or may not in itself create detrimental effects, but the implementation of using separate classrooms may create this effect. This problem means that targeting can impose efficiency and equity costs in the process of otherwise trying to increase progressivity and limit direct program costs.

Many advocates and researchers are encouraging a broader approach to serving children with and without disabilities. Labeling on the basis of disabilities is less important when attention is directed toward the function and the environment, and away from the individual, leading back to more universal rather than targeted programs. Thus, if a truly "appropriate" education is provided to *all* children, then those with disabilities would automatically be served in an appropriate manner. Ensuring that buildings and other public accommodations are physically accessible shifts focus away from any one individual and toward the environment more generally.

Gradation of Benefits

There are wide variations among individuals in the extent to which they face disadvantages due to mental or physical limitations. In many programs, however, the measurement of disability is used for making thumbs up/thumbs down decisions on eligibility. Relating benefits to needs argues for increasing expenditures among individuals as their needs rise or opportunities fall. This implies that benefits could be gradated according to such criteria. Those with less limiting disabilities, for instance, are not necessarily deserving of zero assistance relative to those with more permanent or total disabilities, even if the two groups are not deserving of the same level of assistance.

> *Those with less limiting disabilities are not necessarily deserving of zero assistance relative to those with more permanent or total disabilities, even if the two groups are not deserving of the same level of assistance.*

There are two dimensions to gradation: eligibility and level of benefit. One could allow for wider variation in who is considered eligible under the disability criteria, including individuals with temporary disabilities or less severe disabilities. Practices among programs vary widely. For example, workers compensation provides benefits to anyone who can show that his or her injury is work-related, including persons with either temporary or permanent disabilities. In contrast,

By way of contrast with SSI and SSDI, workers compensation provides benefits to anyone who can show that his or her injury is work-related, including persons with either temporary or permanent disabilities.

the SSI and SSDI programs restrict benefits to persons who are considered incapable of substantial work, or children with conditions of "comparable severity." Somewhat in the middle of these two approaches is the vocational rehabilitation program which extends potential eligibility to all persons who require services to be able to work. However, when resources are inadequate to serve all persons, priority is given under state vocational rehabilitation programs to persons with the most severe disabilities, provided they are not so disabled as to be unlikely to benefit from these services.

Once eligibility has been determined, benefits could also vary with the severity of the disability or the needs related to each type of disability. For those with oscillating needs, a system that allows for variation in treatment of disability could be especially helpful in limiting problems associated with movement into and out of a status of eligibility due to minor changes in conditions. In addition, benefits can vary with income level. Currently, SSI benefits vary by income level to some extent.

In practice, gradation of benefits presents a number of problems. Accurate differentiation of relative disability or functional limitation may be even more difficult to obtain than are current determinations, and boundary lines may be even more fuzzy. Partial and temporary disabilities pose multiple levels of problems with respect to inclusion and exclusion errors, thus leading to related violations of fairness and efficiency. The cost of an error may be smaller—less will be at stake in moving up or down a scale than onto or off of the scale—but the number of errors typically increases with expansion in both number of eligibles and the multiple types of benefits to be determined. Mashaw notes that nations such as Holland "that have tried public partial disability programs have had very unhappy experiences. The availability of partial awards allows adjudicators to 'give everyone something' in circumstances in which most cases certainly seem deserving of some form of assistance."[11] His comments refer primarily to programs dealing with adults, but may be applicable to children as well.

TYPES OF BENEFITS

Closely related to the issue of who receives benefits is what types of benefits should be provided. Indeed, the issues are sometimes inseparable, as when gradation of benefits affects both eligibility and the level of benefits. Here we focus particularly on choices among different types of benefits and where trade-offs in principles are involved. Should benefits emphasize investment in the individual or basic support which usually is more progressive? What is the efficiency trade-off between providing benefits in cash or in-kind, such as educational or medical?

Investment versus Support

Children with disabilities have immediate needs, such as food, shelter, and medical care, as well as more specific developmental needs, such as education and vocational habilitation. Benefits can be aimed at basic support or at enabling persons with disabilities to develop their work or social skills. Chapter 2 makes clear that the majority of expenditures for children with disabilities are aimed at investment for the future—in education or other services that help each individual improve in his or her capacity to later achieve independent living, community integration, participation in the workforce, and other long-term goals.

> *The majority of expenditures for children with disabilities are aimed at investment for the future—in education, vocational services, or other services. These tend to be more investment-oriented than spending on adults with disabilities.*

The break between support and investment is not clean. Some supportive expenditures may have investment value and vice-versa. Children who are ill, or whose basic needs are unmet, are unable to study. Expenditures on food and shelter provide a base from which children develop. Early provision of supports such as prenatal or infant care can reduce the need for future services by forestalling additional disabilities or improving a child's condition. In addition, direct support in the form of cash can reduce government costs by enabling a family member to stay home with the child, thus avoiding or reducing expensive residential placement or the need for home care services.

The returns from educational investment are generally less progressive than are simple cash transfers: the largest payoff is usually to those who learn the most, not necessarily those who have the most to learn.

Expenditures on investment, nonetheless, tend to be distributed differently than supportive expenditures. Because the former emphasize individual development and measure program effectiveness in those terms, they tend to relate benefits to both need and opportunity. Investment returns to education, for example, are sometimes highest where the disability is less severe, where the individual and family are highly motivated, or where the investment is most likely to reduce dependence on others. The returns from educational investment, moreover, are generally less progressive in their ultimate distribution than are simple cash transfers: the larger payoff is usually to those who learn more and will eventually have higher lifetime earnings, not necessarily to those who have the most to learn.

Spending on children with disabilities tends to be much more investment-oriented than spending on adults with disabilities. Cash payments under SSI and Social Security Disability Insurance (SSDI) are a much larger fraction of total support of adults and are much more likely to support consumption than education or other investment.

That educational expenditures in general are not oriented preponderantly to the most disadvantaged in society is reflected in the view that *everyone* should receive an "appropriate" education. This investment orientation stresses that education for everyone enhances growth, which in turn enhances the well-being of all—through better products, improvements in health, and higher future taxes to support

> *Investment orientation stresses that education for everyone enhances growth, which in turn enhances the well-being of all.*

future social programs. Prevention efforts—those that reduce the number of persons who are disabled in the future and the severity of their disabilities—may also be viewed as investments that compete partially with programs aimed at more basic support.

In-kind versus Cash Benefits

Whether programs should provide in-kind benefits or cash historically has been one of the most contentious, yet unresolved, issues of social policy. There are multiple trade-offs involved here, often among different types of efficiency gains. For families of children with disabilities, the most flexible benefit is cash provided by the SSI program.

> *Provision of cash benefits gives greatest choice and discretion to families, but is not always spent in a manner considered appropriate by the public.*

Once declared eligible, the family is given a cash payment with no restrictions on its use, except that it must be used for the child's benefit. It may be used to provide needed services for the child, basic family support, respite assistance, or to serve some purpose unrelated to the disability of the child. Provision of cash benefits, therefore, gives greatest choice and discretion to families and may allow resources to be used more effectively and efficiently—at least as the parents or guardians define it.

Cash assistance, however, is not always spent in a manner considered appropriate by the public, or most efficient in promoting the best interests of the child with a disability. In theory, the justification for a higher level of payment under SSI than other welfare programs is that the differential is related to the additional costs imposed by the disability. This implies that the funds should be spent to help meet those differential costs. Although SSI cash payments must be used for the child's benefit, they do not necessarily need to be spent for a disability-related need. Furthermore, enforcement of how these benefits are actually used is virtually nonexistent. Providing in-kind benefits is one way to ensure that only those services that are deemed appropriate by the public are publicly subsidized.[12]

Although SSI cash payments must be used for the child's benefit, they do not necessarily need to be spent for a disability-related need.

Most program expenditures for children with disabilities fund in-kind benefits. The largest programs, special education and Medicaid, provide in-kind services directly, usually without any form of intermediary payment to the family or individual. These types of in-kind programs, where the government pays providers directly rather than supplying some type of funding controlled by the beneficiary, have often turned out to be costly.

A major reason for this high cost is that part of the outlays is captured by providers, such as health care providers, teachers, and administrators. In many government programs, individuals demand services without full consideration of costs, while providers bargain with government over salaries or fees without full consideration of the demands of clients. Depending upon the design of assistance programs, providers often will charge and provide what the market will bear. For example, to care for an infant with severe disabilities may be quite costly if highly-paid surgeons spend significant time providing services. As a second example, providers are often paid at a set rate per hour or day. One consequence is that they have an incentive to provide services over a longer time than may be strictly needed, a possibility that is reinforced by the lack of objective criteria determining the amount of services that would be most cost-beneficial. Finally, government provision of specific in-kind services will often begin to replace some services previously paid for by other means. In particular, unpaid family care and volunteer services provided outside the family may decline. Medical services previously supplied at low or zero cost will be billed at full rates.

One alternative to both direct service provision and cash benefits is the voucher. Vouchers give families access to a specified dollar amount for particular services. These systems give choice to families over specific service providers, but limit the amount of spending and the purposes to which the funds can be directed. The Food Stamp Program provides a monthly dollar amount of vouchers ("stamps") to families that can only be redeemed for food items. Some states have implemented voucher systems for education, where families are allowed a specified dollar amount to spend on educational services.[13]

In recent years, there has been movement toward "empowerment" of families over their service plans and allowing families greater flexibility, including choice of service providers. A voucher system for respite care, for example, can allow families to determine when to use a service, who provides it, and the methods that are used. This system can attain greater efficiency through family choice while limiting benefits to a specified range of goods and services.

A voucher system can attain greater efficiency through family choice while limiting benefits to a specific service.

In practice, there remain many problems in trying to implement in-kind voucher-type programs. Deciding on the type of in-kind care to provide (e.g., respite care versus recreational activities versus better equipment versus clothing) can be crucial. Even with targeted vouchers, in-kind benefits still create a risk of over-use of some services that would not have been used to the same extent under a cash program, and under-use of some important services that are not covered under the in-kind program. This problem is particularly complex when there is great variation in need across families.

Any in-kind system, even one of vouchers, will have to rely on some level of regulation. In addition to determining which services are allowable, decisions must be made about which providers and products are "certified" under the program, whether to reimburse families or pay providers directly, and how to assure access to services that are provided.

One means to provide further flexibility, yet not move fully to cash, is to offer what we call "structured choice."[14] Structured choice allows

Structured choice allows recipients to choose among a greater variety of alternatives than a simple voucher for one type of good or service, but still does not go all the way toward cash.

recipients to choose among a greater variety of alternatives than a simple voucher for one type of good or service, but still does not go all the way toward cash. Structured choice can be designed either as a voucher that covers a variety of alternatives, or as a grant that will be made only upon approval of some intermediary, such as a government or nonprofit institution. In one sense, this approach is closely related to the individualized service plans being used in educational and other settings and shares the flexibility that such plans can provide. Several states have begun to create family support programs, on a small scale, using a variety of structured choice strategies that limit spending to a certain subset of items and services.[15] Structured choice may be a way to gain the efficiencies of family control of resources while not losing the public desire to limit benefits to certain spheres.

INCENTIVES FOR DECISION-MAKERS

For society as a whole, the cost of a social program cannot be measured simply by the size of the transfer. After all, the cost to the transferor is a benefit to the transferee. When individuals distort their behavior in response to the incentives and disincentives created by a program, however, there are additional costs—efficiency losses—to society that are not balanced out by benefits elsewhere. The actions of families, recipients, administrators, and policymakers in different jurisdictions are all affected by program rules and design. The incentives they confront, while often the unintended results of the way that programs are designed to meet certain goals, feed back to affect efficiency and equity of the programs themselves. Although our focus is again on programs for children with disabilities, many of the incentives we discuss are common to other social programs.

Incentives for Recipients and their Families

Despite the best of intentions, some provisions in programs for children with disabilities can work against stated goals and the long-term well-being of the child. Disincentives to work, save, and prepare for the future, in particular, encourage dependency even while the programs ideally seek to promote independence. Families of children with disabilities are put in the unhappy position of having to forgo activities that would be in their children's best interest in order to receive program benefits which the parent sees as critical to the child and family's well-being.

Means-tested programs, such as SSI and Medicaid, create perverse work disincentives through high "tax rates" on earnings.

Means-tested programs, such as SSI, Medicaid, Food Stamps and rental assistance, create perverse work disincentives through high "tax rates" on earnings. In addition to normal income and social security taxes, beneficiaries find that many of their government benefits are reduced or eliminated as their income increases, thus reducing the benefits of working. Because some portion of parental income is considered in eligibility for SSI and Medicaid, this work disincentive applies to parents, as well as to children who are old enough to work.

Losses of benefits are really nothing more than additional tax systems imposed on those categorically eligible for the means-tested benefits. These tax rates are often quite high. In a comprehensive analysis of all programs affecting AFDC recipients, Giannarelli and Steuerle found combined tax rates in excess of 70 percent for earnings from part-time minimum-wage jobs up through full-time jobs at two to three times minimum wage.[16] And these figures do not include added costs of working such as transportation and child care. The "tax rates" in the SSI program, especially when combined with other programs, are likely to be similar—or even higher, where the value or cost of health insurance is above average. An equally thorough examination of this population, however, has not been performed.

Programs such as SSI and Medicaid limit the amount of assets allowable. This disincentive to save is particularly problematic for children with disabilities who will continue to have financial needs throughout their lives.

These perverse disincentives are a consequence of separate attempts both to increase progressivity and to minimize costs. Program dollars can be concentrated at the lowest income levels only by imposing extremely high tax rates on anyone who moves beyond those income levels. Thus, efforts to increase progressivity and minimize costs for taxpayers—worthwhile goals in and of themselves—can create disincentives to work, as well as lead to a general sense of unfairness for recipients, their families, and those near eligibility cut-offs. Of course, the magnitude of the disincentive to work caused by high tax rates needs to be considered when balancing the costs of this disincentive against the benefits of progressivity and lower expenditures. Thus, higher expenditures may raise tax rates on non-recipients. At the same time, the effect on behavior is an important consideration. While the magnitude in programs for children with disabilities is not known, studies of the AFDC program suggest the effect on work behavior is either small or very hard to measure.

Many means-tested programs such as SSI and Medicaid also limit the amount of resources or assets allowable to recipients. This disincentive to save is particularly problematic for those children with disabilities who will continue to have financial needs throughout their lives. Current SSI rules generally allow for not more than $2,000 in assets excluding a house, a car, and parents' pension funds. However, recognizing this potential disincentive, the SSI program allows exclusions from eligibility calculations of income or resources that are set aside as part of an approved plan to achieve self-support (PASS), including funds for education, vocational training, or to start a business. This option is only used infrequently because of administrative complexity and the generally low income levels of SSI recipients and their families. However, the recognition of saving disincentives allows for similar options to be adopted.

Programs with disability eligibility criteria can also create a disincentive to invest in the future by preparing for work or learning work-readiness skills. If a child is involved in steps that help prepare him or her for an independent future, the child may no longer qualify under the disability standards. Note that the problem is more severe the less likely the child is to achieve significant income as a result of work preparation. That is, attaining a higher level of productivity that moves one just beyond assistance levels is often likely to result in little or no gain in income, so the loss of benefits is quite threatening. For those who can move well beyond assistance, on the other hand, the gains are likely to be substantial. For both groups, the connection of Medicaid eligibility to SSI eligibility provides special disincentives to parents who fear that their children will be unable to pay future medical bills without Medicaid.

Still another example of negative incentives is that parents can be forced to compromise the best care alternatives for their child in order

---

The connection of Medicaid eligibility to SSI eligibility provides special disincentives to parents who fear that their children will be unable to pay future medical bills without Medicaid.

---

to get any care. SSI rules at one time made it easier for children to receive SSI, and therefore Medicaid, if the child was in an institutional setting rather than at home. Parental income is not included in determining SSI eligibility for children in most institutional settings. Although SSI cash benefits are minimal in this situation, children are then eligible for Medicaid automatically in most states. This set of incentives discouraged what not only may be the most appropriate care, but also what is usually the least expensive form of care: in the home. Changes in the Medicaid program, starting with the "Katie Beckett" provision, were made to allow children to retain Medicaid eligibility if receiving care at home, as long as the costs to Medicaid do not exceed those of institutional care. This is another example of program design attempting to overcome unintended disincentives.

The types of disincentives described here are to some extent inherent in any program using means-testing and disability criteria to target eligible populations. More universal programs that are not means-tested avoid many of these problems. However, as noted, universal programs usually entail higher costs and less progressivity. Another more universal strategy is to focus program efforts on providing in-kind benefits that target habilitation or developmental services.

Incentives for Administrators

In a world where need is difficult to measure and disability determinations involve some level of subjectivity, the motivations and incentives of administrators must also be examined and taken into account. On the one hand, human psychology almost inevitably leads each of us to want to help others. This implies that those working in and administering disability programs probably have strong internal motivations to want to help. As a society we would not want it to be any other way. Where dividing lines are hard to draw and determinations open to subjective judgments, therefore, there probably are strong tendencies toward inclusion if at all possible. This incentive applies to physicians, social workers, and all others involved in presenting or examining information used in disability determinations. Where budgets are limited, on the other hand, the tendency may be to include those already eligible, but to exclude any new category of eligibles, no matter what their relative needs. We understand, for instance, that this may be the practice in many school systems in setting priorities in special education.

Where eligibility criteria are complicated, such as the disability criteria in SSI, different environments may also produce very different outcomes. In Part II, we present significant differences by state in the proportion of children eligible for national disability programs and in growth rates of programs whose eligibility criteria were changing. An administrator working in a system defined by legal boundaries may be pulled in different directions: first, trying to reach consistency with the standards operating in that jurisdiction, but then trying not to vary too much from "common" practices, as determined in part by the actions in other jurisdictions.

Where administrative decision-making tends to be expansive in nature, the consequences are not always the best for the most severely disabled. When all eligibles receive the same benefits and definitions of eligibility are expanded, simple mathematics shows that a greater *share* of resources goes to those with less severe problems. Sometimes the more severely disabled later receive lower benefits, not just a reduced share. If budget constraints lead to program cuts that are imposed on all beneficiaries equally—as when benefits are capped—the net result is likely to be fewer benefits for those with the most severe disabilities.

As in all administrative systems, mechanisms for enforcement and handling appeal processes require that documentation of decision criteria be made. Resources available to carry out eligibility determinations, however, are limited. While there are necessary reasons for documentation, the quality of service received and the quality of the determination itself may not always be related to the precision of the documentation, especially when the latter is geared to legal considerations. Administrator flexibility might lead to more efficient use of resources, but it will be greatly limited in a system facing continuous legal action based on documentation.

Administrator flexibility might lead to more efficient use of resources, but it will be greatly limited in a system facing continuous legal action based on documentation.

As one example of the interplay between program structures and administrator incentives, special education programs are required to develop and implement an individualized educational plan (IEP) for each student needing special education services. These plans can include many services in addition to direct educational services. Although the school system is required by law to provide an appropriate education (consistent with information in the IEP), there are significant pressures on administrators to exclude expensive services from some students IEPs in order to avoid overburdening the school or school district financially.

Incentives by Jurisdiction

In a federal system, different jurisdictions may face very different sets of incentives for reforming or administering programs for children with disabilities. When a program is jointly funded at different levels of government, an unintended by-product is that no one governmental entity takes into account the full range of benefits and costs due to any reform. For example, in a matching program, a state might only save 50 cents for each dollar garnered by the program through tighter eligibility requirements. Similarly, it will cost it only 50 cents to increase beneficiary payments by a dollar. In economic terms, no entity "internalizes" decision-making by taking into consideration all the benefits and costs relevant to the particular trade-offs at hand.

When programs face different mixes of incentives, there are strong interaction effects. For example, states match federal funds in programs like AFDC, while SSI is almost entirely funded by the federal government, giving state or program administrators incentives to encourage needy persons to qualify under SSI rather than AFDC. After all, such a move may increase benefits for the recipient at little or no cost to the state. If either the state or the federal government was entirely responsible for both programs, different decisions might be made by either one in setting and administering policy.

States match federal funds in programs like AFDC, while SSI is almost entirely funded by the federal government, giving state or program administrators incentives to encourage needy persons to qualify for SSI rather than AFDC.

In addition to these incentives, state and local control over programs may lead to greater efficiency, given the varying needs across geographic areas coupled with greater knowledge about local needs and demands. This can also mean that experimentation in program design and implementation may yield the greatest rewards where there is state or local control. Redistributing resources to relate benefits progressively to needs across states, however, is less possible when states oversee programs. Another potential disadvantage of state or local control over program structure is more unequal treatment of individuals in equal situations in different parts of the nation.

Any program configuration will likely create incentives for decision-makers, families, administrators, or jurisdictions, that are contrary to some established program goals. The incentives discussed here represent only some of the more obvious and important ones under the current system. However, the consequences are more likely to be perverse if they are unintended and not understood. In designing programs, the balance between program goals and unwanted disincentives—including the effect of those disincentives on sectoral behavior—needs to considered explicitly.

CONCLUSIONS

Americans have aspired to secure participation, independence, and opportunity for individuals with disabilities through both private actions and public legislation. While much progress has been made, the nation still struggles to achieve these and other worthy societal goals more fully. Budget considerations and changing approaches to providing services are causing programs to be carefully examined. Enacting reform in ways that meet the needs of children with disabilities and that are effective and sensible for them, their families, and society, however, is not simple.

To foster systematic thinking about programs serving children with disabilities, we have suggested first viewing these programs as a whole and then assessing potential future changes through use of a set of commonly shared principles. We have offered five principles particularly helpful when relating goals to resources: directing benefits toward needs; assuring fairness and equity among individuals in equal circumstances; supporting individual development; assuring that resources are spent well; and relating benefits to contributions.

Although these principles reflect commonly accepted notions of fairness, efficiency, and individual development, they can and often do conflict with one another. In these instances, compromises and trade-offs must be made, and one must judge the relative importance of each principal in context. While these principles, therefore, are unlikely to yield easy answers on how to allocate resources, they are still powerful in helping to "frame" or bound reasonable sets of policy alternatives.

The many difficult choices faced by policymakers include determining: who should be eligible for programs, the level of inclusion or exclusion errors that is tolerable, whether to limit benefits to certain income or disability groups, whether benefits should be aimed at development or basic support, and the form of the benefit (cash, in-kind, or something in-between such as structured choice). These choices can be best addressed—i.e., their benefits and costs best weighed—only by a systematic consideration of how each choice falls from or violates a basic set of principles. In addition, policymakers should be aware of how efficiency and fairness are affected by the incentive structures faced by beneficiaries, administrators, and different jurisdictions.

Notes

1. Jerry Mashaw, "Disability: Why Does the Search for Good Programs Continue?" In James Schulz and Eric Kingston (eds.), *Social Security in the 21st Century*, forthcoming.

2. For those who base their choices on a guiding paradigm of moral obligation of society or right of the individual, the amount of transfer required is that necessary to fulfill the obligation. Implicitly the amount of transfer is still related to need, here determined by the specific right or obligation in question. As long as a society falls short of full equality or full attainment of all such rights, however, even this strong version of the progressivity principle is inadequate by itself to assess how to allocate existing resources. One still requires principles and guidelines to allocate the limited resources that are made available and to deal with multiple claims of rights and obligations. For a given individual, for instance, rights to both health care and access to transportation might be claimed. Among individuals, an appropriate educational opportunity might be sought for both the student with disabilities and the student with other economic and social disadvantages.

3. Progressivity is sometimes sought by transferring more from those with greater means, not by paying higher benefits to those in greater need. Universal programs such as Old Age and Survivors Insurance (OASI) in Social Security are often examples.

4. Steuerle and Bakija demonstrate that many of the benefits to individuals in OASI and DI cannot be justified under this principle, as the insurance value of benefits is often well in excess of the value of premiums or taxes contributed by individuals. Historically, for instance, many high-income individuals received the largest OASI transfers, defined as benefits in excess of taxes paid. See C. Eugene Steuerle, and Jon M. Bakija, *Retooling Social Security for the 21st Century: Right and Wrong Approaches to Reform*, Urban Institute Press, Washington, D.C., 1994 and Jon M. Bakija and C. Eugene Steuerle, "Social Security Disability Insurance: Fiscal Imbalance and Lifetime Value," Urban Institute, Washington, D.C., 1995.

5. Steuerle and Bakija argue that wage replacement should not be viewed as a principle, but only an application of this individual equity principle. Wage replacement generally cannot be justified on a need-based or progressivity principle alone, as there are likely to be equal or greater needs in society than replacing the wages of a higher-income person. On the other hand, if contributions rise with wages, society may accept the individual equity of granting all individuals a fair return on their insurance contributions and premiums. See Steuerle and Bakija, *Retooling Social Security for the 21st Century*, 1994.

6. When comparing government programs, these principles compel one to consider whether investment in children represents long-term societal investments and whether children's relative needs are reflected in their high poverty rates and their limited ability to support themselves. By the same token, the disadvantages and needs of children are not a function of disabilities alone; moreover, programs serving children

will compete with programs where individuals claim a right to some return on prior "contributions." While a broader comparison of all government expenditure programs is beyond the scope of this study, any redesign of programs for children with disabilities should take such considerations into account.

7. General Accounting Office, "Social Security: New Functional Assessments for Children Raise Eligibility Questions," GAO/HEHS-95-66, Washington, D.C., March 1995.

8. Note that this universality in special education services mirrors the provision of a free public education to all the nation's children. Indeed, many children with disabilities are served through general education programs in addition to receiving special education services.

9. For these reasons, the income tax allows deductions of extraordinary medical expenses, including those due to disabilities, from the measure of income subject to tax.

10. For a thorough treatment of this issue, see Nicholas Hobbs, *The Futures of Children: Categories, Labels, and Their Consequences*, Jossey-Bass, San Francisco, 1975.

11. Jerry Mashaw, "Disability," forthcoming.

12. Note that these types of concerns are rarely raised in discussions of disabled *adult* SSI beneficiaries. This is largely because, for adults, the SSI benefit is thought to replace lost wages (which are usually spent in any way the earner chooses). A similar argument can be made with respect to lost family wages in the case of children with disabilities, which is an additional motivation for SSI payments to children.

13. The more liquid the voucher, the more it operates like cash. Food stamps, for instance, are closer to cash than are educational vouchers, which cannot as easily be sold or transferred to others.

14. C. Eugene Steuerle, "Uses of the Negative Income Tax Framework," *Focus*, 12(3): 30–32, Spring 1990.

15. For a discussion of some of these state programs see Valerie Bradley, James Knoll, and John Agosta, *Emerging Issues in Family Support*, AAMR Monographs, 1992.

16. Linda Giannarelli and C. Eugene Steuerle, "The Twice Poverty Trap: Tax Rates Faced by AFDC Recipients," The Urban Institute, Washington, D.C., April 1995.

Part Two

DETAILED PROGRAM DESCRIPTIONS

Chapter Four

GOVERNMENT PROGRAMS SERVING CHILDREN WITH DISABILITIES

This chapter reviews the major government programs benefiting children with disabilities at the federal, state, and local levels in 1995. The discussion highlights the largest programs: Supplemental Security Income (SSI), Medicaid, Parts B and H of Individuals with Disabilities Education Act (IDEA), Maternal and Child Health Block Grants, state mental retardation/developmental disability (MR/DD) programs, state mental health programs, Head Start, and state family support programs.

Partly because of the way that programs for children with disabilities are designed and administered, there is a tendency for policymakers, researchers, and administrators to know a great deal about one program and little about others. As the purpose of this study is to encourage systematic thinking about the programs combined, one focus is to bring together for the first time information about each of the programs in one place. Thus, this study makes it possible for someone working in, say, education to see how policy choices in health and cash assistance programs also may come into play in the lives of the children they are serving.

The current period is obviously one of potentially large changes for programs serving children with disabilities. The federal budget crunch is placing pressure, large by historical standards, on almost all expenditure programs. Political realignments also alter the levels of commitment of new decision-makers to the policy designs of their predecessors. Federalism—block grants, devolution, entitlements, the appropriate roles for different levels of government—can be expected to remain an issue for many years to come. And programs for children with disabilities cannot help but feel some of the impact of this debate. Indeed, one of the major purposes of this study was to provide a broader base against which changes could be considered by those active in this discussion, including a federal commission established to examine Supplemental Security Income (SSI) for children with disabilities. We remain more convinced than ever that these changes cannot be made well if each program is weighed in isolation. More than an issue of money, many programs' purpose, eligibility criteria, and administration will be under examination for years, and must be considered in relation to the whole.

To gauge the appropriateness of SSI cash benefits for children with disabilities, for example, policymakers must fully assess the advantages and disadvantages of changing eligibility criteria, of converting cash benefits into services or vouchers, and of devolving responsibility to states. These choices, in turn, require that one know what services are available through other programs and who is eligible. What educational and health benefits might otherwise be provided? To what extent does eligibility for SSI affect eligibility for health care benefits such as Medicaid? And if the systems are changed dramatically, how will new programs of cash support relate to educational and health programs? An accounting of the programs currently in place informs policy and program development by demonstrating the various ways these questions have been approached to date.

In truth, change is almost always evolutionary rather than revolutionary. Even when programs are actually eliminated in name, they are often replaced with other programs that serve similar purposes and many of the same families. Those things that administrators know how to do, or do well, they often repeat in any new setting. Thus, we would be surprised if there were short-term, wholesale changes in families served, the share of benefits paid in the form of education or health, or other major characteristics of the system as a whole.

If significant changes do occur, it becomes more important than ever that a benchmark be established. Without any thorough accounting of existing programs, it would be difficult, if not impossible, to determine how large or important were the changes that took place— except by anecdote. The review of programs presented here, therefore, also serves as the only comprehensive, contemporary benchmark against which future program changes and refinements might be measured. To this end, this review also provides, to the extent possible, important historical information on trends over time in program participation and funding levels, to which future data can be added. We also hope that policy development can benefit from better information and data collection. See Appendix D for preliminary recommendations.

Finally, it is important to remember the basic reason that current programs exist—to meet needs of children and families. These needs remain regardless of the ways they are met or not met, e.g., through a larger or smaller number of programs, or through administration at the federal, state, or local levels. A systematic review of programs reveals just how society has attempted in all its fallibility to meet these needs so far. Most of the problems of existing programs—the tradeoffs they face, the difficulty of measurement, the creation of disincentives—will not go away simply because new labels and administrative designs are attached to these programs or their replacements.

For each major program serving children with disabilities that follows, we include a description of the types of services provided, general eligibility requirements, and administration. Programs vary in their definitions of disability and use different eligibility criteria, partly because of the many purposes and intents of different programs. We also detail participation in and expenditures by each program. Where possible, these figures are reported over time, in total, and by subgroups (such as type of disability and demographic characteristics).

Many other programs that serve children with disabilities are not reviewed here, but few of those excluded have eligibility criteria based upon disability. Examples of these excluded programs are Food Stamps, Aid to Families with Dependent Children (AFDC), foster care and child welfare programs, housing subsidies, and most primary and secondary education. For these programs, it is not usually possible to separate out expenditures for children with disabilities. Furthermore, these programs would be available to children regardless of their disability status. A few other programs that are targeted to children with disabilities are not included either because they are small, or, like Vocational Rehabilitation, are focused mainly on the transition to adulthood.[1]

SUPPLEMENTAL SECURITY INCOME

The Supplemental Security Income (SSI) program is a federally administered program providing cash benefits to poor persons who are aged, blind, or disabled. Children under the age of 18 (or up to age 22 for full-time students) who meet the eligibility requirements for disability and whose families' income and resources fall below the eligibility threshold are eligible for SSI benefits.

The SSI program began in 1974 and replaced state-administered programs such as the Aid to the Blind program, established by the Social Security Act of 1935. The programs were run by the states with federal matching funds. Eligibility and benefit levels varied by state. The programs were mainly for the poor and eligibility was restricted to adults. Children from low-income families with disabilities were usually included in states' AFDC programs. The SSI program was created to provide supplemental income to poor elderly individuals and to federalize the state programs for the needy blind and disabled. Unlike the state programs which preceded it, SSI also provided benefits to children under 18.

Prior to SSI, federal programs for persons with disabilities or the aged, including Social Security's Old Age Survivors Insurance (OASI) and Disability Insurance (SSDI), were insurance programs with the primary goal of insuring against the inability to work due to age or disability. The reason for including children under SSI, as opposed to some other program less related to work, is not completely clear. Most likely, it was a convenient vehicle at the time. The House Ways and Means Committee's original report on the SSI legislation states that needy blind and disabled children were included because they were "certainly among the most disadvantaged of all Americans" and "deserved special assistance in order to help them become self-supporting members of our society."[2]

Eligibility

To qualify for SSI, children with disabilities must meet both medical and financial eligibility requirements. In the SSI statute, the disability eligibility requirement is defined as being "unable to engage in any substantial gainful activity by reason of any medically determined physical or mental impairment which can be expected to result in death or which has lasted or can be expected to last for a continuous period of not less than 12 months (or, in the case of a child under the age of 18, if he suffers from any medically determinable physical or mental impairment of comparable severity)" (P.L. 92-603).[3] The traditional use of the term "substantial gainful activity" was mainly relevant for adults; children who have an impairment of "comparable severity" to eligible adults are, nonetheless, considered disabled. There has been much controversy over the interpretation of "comparable severity" and the process by which children are evaluated.

In February 1990, the Supreme Court decision in *Sullivan v. Zebley* found that SSI's approach to determining disability for children was not comparable to the approach used for adults. Social Security Administration (SSA) regulations provide specific criteria for determining disability eligibility. Prior to the *Zebley* decision, the first step in the SSI disability determination process involved assessing whether the child or adult had an impairment that met (or equaled the severity of) the impairments and conditions listed by the Social Security Administration. This list of conditions differed for adults and children, but included conditions of comparable severity. In addition, adults not deemed eligible through this route were given an individual assessment. The individual assessment determined whether an adult had an impairment which prevented him or her from being able to work. Children who did not have a condition meeting the medical listing were not given an individual assessment. The Zebley decision found the lack of an assessment process for children in violation of the original statute.

In response to the Zebley decision, the Social Security Administration now includes an individual functional assessment (IFA) for children who do not meet the first disability criteria of having an impairment (or one of comparable severity) listed in SSA's medical standard. Because inability to work could not be used as the standard in the children's assessment, the new regulations define the IFA standard as "having an impairment or combination of impairments that substantially reduce the child's ability to grow, develop, or mature physically, mentally, or emotionally" and thus to "function independently, appropriately, and effectively in an age-appropriate manner." The areas considered in an IFA include social, communication, cognitive, and motor skills. The skills considered vary somewhat by the age of the child. As part of the Zebley decision, the Social Security Administration agreed to reconsider under the new criteria, all child eligibility determinations made between January 1980 and February 1991 (when the new regulations were put in place).

An additional change in eligibility determination for children was the broadening of the medical listings by the Disability Benefits Reform Act of 1984 (DBRA). In December 1990, in accordance with the DBRA, the Social Security Administration revised and expanded the list of eligible mental impairments for children to reflect changes in medical technology and terminology. The new listings for mental impairments are also more functionally based, relating the impairment to the child's ability to carry out age-appropriate activities. These standards add new specific mental impairments, such as attention deficit hyperactivity disorder and psychoactive substance dependence disorders, to the list of eligible conditions.[4]

SSI recipients must also meet financial eligibility requirements. Income must be below a specified threshold, or benefit standard, to qualify for SSI. In January 1995, the federal benefit standard for an individual is $458 of monthly income. To be eligible, resources (or assets) must not exceed $2,000. For a child under the age of 18 who meets the medical criteria, a portion of the parents' income and resources are "deemed" to be available to the child. Parents can exclude from the resources used in calculating eligibility a home, a car used for necessary transportation, and parents' pension funds. The child's income plus income deemed from parents (less allowable exclusions and deductions) is compared to the benefit standard; the difference is the federal SSI benefit.

SSI is a program of "last resort"—that is, it counts income from other sources, including cash assistance programs such as AFDC and Social Security, in determining eligibility. In-kind assistance from many federal and state programs, such as Medicaid and Food Stamps, is not counted.

Children who reside in a public medical facility for which Medicaid will pay more than 50 percent of costs are eligible for a minimal monthly SSI payment of $30. Although this personal allowance payment is small, SSI eligibility is highly valued because in many states SSI recipients are automatically eligible for Medicaid. Also, children in residential facilities for more than 30 days do not have parental income deemed to them in the calculation of SSI eligibility.

AFDC AND SSI

An individual cannot receive both SSI and AFDC payments. However, a family can receive AFDC for other family members, while a child (or parent) receives SSI. An individual who is eligible for both programs can choose which one to receive. While individuals will qualify for different benefit levels under each program and there is variation across states in AFDC benefit levels and state supplementation of SSI, generally SSI provides a larger benefit than AFDC. For a sample of children receiving SSI, the Inspector General reports that 58 percent were receiving AFDC at the time of application to SSI. Children in families that receive no income other than AFDC, however, have SSI benefits reduced by one-third.[5]

In some states there is a financial incentive for the state to encourage individuals to receive SSI rather than AFDC, because SSI is a federally paid benefit while AFDC is a state-paid benefit with a federal match. In some states, however, the state share of the AFDC payment for an additional child may be less than the state supplemental payment for a child on SSI, although both payments are typically small.

Administration

For federal SSI payments, local Social Security Administration offices determine applicants' financial eligibility. Medical eligibility is established by state disability determination services (DDSs) which are funded through a contract and overseen by SSA. The process of appealing benefit denials is similar for all SSI and SSDI applicants. Multiple levels of administrative appeals are possible. The first level is a reconsideration by staff at the DDS agency. The second level of appeal is to an administrative law judge (ALJ) and the final is to the Appeals Council. If the application is denied by the Appeals Council, a civil suit can be brought within 60 days.

STATE SUPPLEMENTAL SSI PROGRAMS

The SSI program consists of federal payments and supplemental state payments. Although the federal program is uniform across all states, state SSI supplementation eligibility criteria and payment levels vary, with some states not providing supplemental payments at all.[6] In 1994, 43 states and the District of Columbia provide optional supplementation benefits to some SSI recipients, and 34 states and the District of Columbia provide a supplemental benefit to some eligible children (Table 4.1). Six of these states provide benefits only to children who are blind. The maximum benefit level for children varies across and within states depending primarily on living arrangements. For example, several states provide supplements only to children who are in residential facilities, and who therefore receive minimal federal SSI payments.

The federal government administers state supplemental payments for 17 states and the District of Columbia. These states must adhere to certain federal criteria. One difficulty in analyzing SSI expenditure data is that the Social Security Administration does not collect information from state-administered programs.

Benefits/Services

SSI provides monthly cash payments to eligible recipients. The level of benefits depends on the income and assets of the child's family. The maximum allowable federal SSI benefit is $458 a month in 1995 for an individual adult or child. While the actual benefit varies with income, of all child SSI recipients, 68 percent received the maximum federal payment and 88 percent received over $300 in January 1995.

Table 4.1 STATE SSI SUPPLEMENTATION PROGRAMS: ELIGIBILITY FOR BLIND
AND DISABLED CHILDREN AND PAYMENTS ADMINISTRATION,
DECEMBER 1994

State	Eligibility of Blind and Disabled Children for State SSI Payments	Administration of State SSI Payments	Average Federally Administered Monthly Payment
Alabama	yes	state	$411.85
Alaska	no	state	395.40
Arizona	yes	state	411.21
Arkansas	no program	no program	409.11
California	yes	federal	489.16
Colorado	yes	state	399.14
Connecticut	blind only	state	408.15
Delaware	no*	federal	383.66
District of Columbia	yes	federal	404.91
Florida	no	state	409.39
Georgia	no program	no program	402.77
Hawaii	yes	federal	378.00
Idaho	yes	state	391.84
Illinois	yes	state	415.18
Indiana	no	state	401.19
Iowa	yes	federal and state	385.41
Kansas	no program	no program	394.99
Kentucky	yes	state	411.92
Louisiana	yes	state	414.16
Maine	yes	federal	388.67
Maryland	no	state	399.70
Massachusetts	yes	federal	446.17
Michigan	yes	federal	414.54
Minnesota	blind only**	state	400.90
Mississippi	no program	no program	412.33
Missouri	no*	state	414.36
Montana	yes	federal	409.11
Nebraska	yes	state	391.63
Nevada	blind only	federal	398.89
New Hampshire	blind only**	state	396.22
New Jersey	yes	federal	427.06

(continued)

Additional eligible children in the family can receive the entire maximum monthly payment: benefits do not decrease with the number of child recipients.[7]

There are no restrictions on how the SSI cash benefits can be spent, other than for the child's benefit. Payments need not be spent on any special needs of the child with disabilities. Representative payees who receive SSI checks on behalf of the eligible child (usually the

Table 4.1 STATE SSI SUPPLEMENTATION PROGRAMS: ELIGIBILITY FOR BLIND
AND DISABLED CHILDREN AND PAYMENTS ADMINISTRATION
(continued)

State	Eligibility of Blind and Disabled Children for State SSI Payments	Administration of State SSI Payments	Average Federally Administered Monthly Payment
New Mexico	yes	state	400.58
New York	yes	federal and state	435.80
North Carolina	blind only	state	397.96
North Dakota	yes	county	377.59
Ohio	no*	state	410.53
Oklahoma	yes	state	410.16
Oregon	blind only	state	395.81
Pennsylvania	yes	federal	435.47
Rhode Island	yes	federal	467.04
South Carolina	no	state	405.01
South Dakota	yes	state	397.88
Tennessee	no program	no program	409.96
Texas	no program	no program	406.14
Utah	yes	federal	393.45
Vermont	yes	federal and state	446.47
Virginia	no	state	398.55
Washington	yes	federal and state	429.30
West Virginia	no program	no program	414.83
Wisconsin	yes	federal	488.70
Wyoming	yes	state	379.50

"No program" means that state does not have an optional SSI supplementation program.
*Blind and disabled children under age 18 are not eligible for payments.
**Disabled children under age 18 are not eligible for payments.
Source: Columns 1 & 2—Office of Supplemental Security Income, *State Assistance Programs for SSI Recipients*, SSA Pub. No. 17-002, January 1994. Column 3—Office of Supplemental Security Income Policy, Social Security Administration, "Children Receiving SSI," December 1994. Data based on a 10-percent sample of SSI recipients for December 1994. Payments include federally administered state supplement payments, but do not include retroactive payments or state administered payments.

parents) are required to submit an annual report on usage of benefits. However, the Inspector General has found that these reports were not always submitted and that they "may deter, but cannot readily detect, misuse of SSI cash payments."[8] In general, SSI benefits are spent on basic needs, such as food and shelter, as well as special needs, such as personal assistance, medical needs, or equipment.

The average federally administered payment varies by state. Table 4.1 (column 4) lists each state's average payment in December 1994 for blind and disabled children, including federally administered state supplementation. The variation across states reflects differences in coverage and payment levels in state programs, variation in federal benefit eligibility, and administration of state payments. The average monthly federally administered SSI payment to children in January 1995 (including federally administered state supplementation) was $421.

OTHER PROGRAM BENEFITS

SSI recipients are eligible for Medicaid coverage in most states. Under SSI law, states have the option of offering Medicaid to all SSI recipients. Thirty-eight states and the District of Columbia have taken this option, covering approximately 79 percent of all SSI recipients in the U.S. Twelve other states offer more restricted eligibility for Medicaid. This is discussed in more detail in the section describing Medicaid.

SSI recipients also have access to direct services from other programs. Until 1981, the SSI program required that certain services be made available to child beneficiaries. These requirements, known as the SSI/Disabled Children's Program (DCP), required state agencies administering the Title V Maternal and Child Health program to play a coordinating and integrating role. These agencies were required to establish "individual service plans" for children on SSI and monitor these plans as well as provide counseling and referrals. In 1981, the SSI/DCP was repealed and these regulations were rescinded. However, the statement of purpose for Title V still states that a "reasonable proportion" of funding be used to provide rehabilitation services for children under the age of 16 receiving SSI. All new SSI beneficiaries under 16 are referred to the Title V Maternal and Child Health program by state DDS units. New SSI recipients who are aged 16 or older are referred to Vocational Rehabilitation programs for services.[9]

Program Participation

The number of blind and disabled children receiving SSI has increased rapidly over time. In December 1994, almost 893,000 blind and disabled children were receiving SSI benefits (Figure 4.1) or approximately 1.3 percent of all children under 18. This is an increase of more than 162 percent since 1990, the year of the *Zebley* decision. In December 1994, blind and disabled children comprised over 14 percent of all SSI participants compared to only 2 percent of the total SSI caseload when the program started in 1974. Children with disabilities are the fastest growing segment of the SSI population.[10] Note that these increases over time are for the *total caseload* and, therefore,

Figure 4.1 NUMBER OF BLIND AND DISABLED CHILDREN RECEIVING SSI, 1974–1994

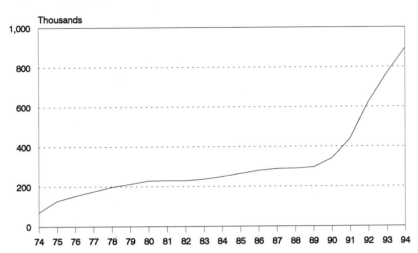

Source: Office of Supplemental Security Income Policy, "Children Receiving SSI," December 1993. Numbers represent caseloads in December of each year.

reflect both changes in the number of new awards and changes in the average length of stay on the program.[11]

The growth in the number of child recipients is a result of large increases in applications, increased awards (successful applications) after the Zebley decision, and the change in the mental impairments listings. Comparing the two-year periods before and after the Zebley decision, the General Accounting Office (GAO) found that average monthly applications for children increased by more than 150 percent. The award rate (the percent of applicants awarded benefits) also increased from 38 percent to 56 percent. In 1992, 31 percent of children who enrolled in SSI were determined eligible on the basis of an individual functional assessment. However, since some of the increase is due to redeterminations of previous denials (a one-time increase), the growth rate may be somewhat lower in the future.[12]

Program changes for children are not the only likely causes of caseload increases; disability caseloads in general have been growing. Figure 4.2 shows SSI adult, child, and aged caseloads as a percent of the relevant population over time. Both adult and child SSI caseloads, which include all individuals eligible due to disability, are increasing. The number of aged (over 65) SSI recipients as a percent of the aged population is declining mainly due to increases in Social Security

Figure 4.2 SSI CASELOAD AS A PERCENTAGE OF THE POPULATION

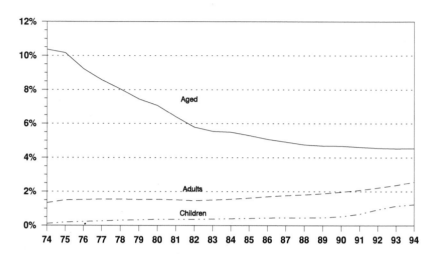

Source: Social Security Administration, Office of Supplemental Security Income Policy, "Children Receiving SSI," December 1994 and U.S. Bureau of the Census, series P25-917, various years. Note: Figures represent caseload divided by respective population. "Aged" represents non-disabled recipients over age 65. "Adults" represents those with disabilities over age 18.

payments. Since 1982, the proportion of adults receiving SSI because of disability has grown steadily from less than 1.5 percent to more than 2 percent of the adult population. Similar growth has occurred in the adult caseload for Social Security Disability Insurance.

The proportion of children receiving SSI varies considerably across states. Table 4.2 shows the total number of child recipients and the number per thousand state residents under age 18 in December 1994. The number of child SSI recipients per thousand children is 13.2 for the United States as a whole. For individual states, this rate varies from about 6.0 in Connecticut and Utah to 32.0 in Louisiana and Mississippi. In general, this variation reflects family incomes in each state, with poorer states having a greater share of children who are financially eligible. The state variation may also reflect differences in disability rates among children across states, which could also be related to family income, education, and family structure.

Table 4.2 also shows growth in caseloads across states from 1989 to 1994. Although federal SSI payments criteria are standard across states, there was significant differences in caseload growth over this period. Total caseload growth for blind and disabled children was 203

Table 4.2 NUMBER OF BLIND AND DISABLED CHILDREN RECEIVING FEDERALLY
ADMINISTERED SSI BY STATE, DECEMBER 1994

State	Number of Blind and Disabled Children Receiving SSI	Number Per Thousand Residents Under 18	Percent Increase 1989–1994
Total	888,470	13.2	+203.0
Alabama	26,910	25.0	226.6
Alaska	720	3.8	100.0
Arizona	10,450	9.8	188.7
Arkansas	18,730	29.5	267.3
California	67,320	7.8	143.1
Colorado	8,710	9.3	154.7
Connecticut	4,860	6.3	135.9
Delaware	2,150	12.3	141.6
District of Columbia	2,530	22.0	158.2
Florida	51,880	16.4	282.0
Georgia	25,920	14.1	166.9
Hawaii	950	3.2	106.5
Idaho	3,390	10.2	202.7
Illinois	46,840	15.3	275.9
Indiana	18,170	12.4	198.8
Iowa	6,870	9.4	155.4
Kansas	7,750	11.3	260.5
Kentucky	19,900	20.5	200.2
Louisiana	39,830	32.0	242.5
Maine	2,430	7.9	158.5
Maryland	11,450	9.2	209.5
Massachusetts	14,240	10.2	151.6
Michigan	36,540	14.6	280.2
Minnesota	9,570	7.8	258.4
Mississippi	24,270	32.0	215.6
Missouri	19,600	14.4	221.3
Montana	2,000	8.6	98.0
Nebraska	4,090	9.3	142.0
Nevada	2,370	6.7	172.4

(continued)

percent. However, the growth for individual states ranged from 100 percent (in Alaska) to over 280 percent (in Florida and Michigan). These differences may reflect differences in economic conditions across states over time, changes in disability rates, outreach or information provision, and other state policies.

Some characteristics of SSI blind and disabled child recipients are shown in Table 4.3.[13] Of all child SSI recipients, 21 percent are under 6 years old, 43 percent are 6 to 12 years old, and 36 percent are over

Table 4.2 NUMBER OF BLIND AND DISABLED CHILDREN RECEIVING FEDERALLY
ADMINISTERED SSI BY STATE, DECEMBER 1994 (continued)

State	Number of Blind and Disabled Children Receiving SSI	Number Per Thousand Residents Under 18	Percent Increase 1989–1994
New Hampshire	1,700	6.0	165.6
New Jersey	20,090	10.6	199.0
New Mexico	6,440	13.4	208.1
New York	75,160	16.8	201.2
North Carolina	26,310	15.4	219.7
North Dakota	1,150	6.7	117.0
Ohio	46,740	16.3	242.2
Oklahoma	11,040	12.7	201.6
Oregon	6,590	8.4	202.3
Pennsylvania	39,750	13.8	185.2
Rhode Island	2,540	10.8	128.8
South Carolina	16,340	17.2	180.8
South Dakota	2,600	12.5	143.0
Tennessee	22,560	17.8	198.0
Texas	53,200	10.3	146.3
Utah	4,260	6.4	195.8
Vermont	1,330	9.2	166.0
Virginia	20,220	12.7	268.3
Washington	10,420	7.5	169.3
West Virginia	7,800	18.0	156.6
Wisconsin	20,630	15.4	243.3
Wyoming	1,070	7.8	269.0

Source: 1994 data: Office of Supplemental Security Income Policy, "Children Receiving SSI," December 1994. 1989 data: Lenna Kennedy, "Children Receiving SSI Payments, December 1992," *Social Security Bulletin*, Summer 1993, p. 81. Numbers based on a 10-percent sample of recipients in December. State population estimates for 1993: U.S. Bureau of the Census, Current Population Reports, Series P-25. This table excludes recipients of non-federally administered state SSI supplementation who do not receive federal benefits.

12 years old. A smaller proportion of children under 3 receive SSI than children in the older age groups. More child recipients are male than female, 63 percent compared to 37 percent. A much higher proportion of black children are recipients than white children or Hispanic children. Differences in average income by race are a contributing factor to these rates.

The vast majority of these children live in their parents' household. About 16 percent are categorized as living in their "own household" for purposes of payment determination, meaning that only the child's

Table 4.3 CHARACTERISTICS OF BLIND AND DISABLED CHILDREN RECEIVING
SSI, DECEMBER 1994

Characteristic	Number of Child Recipients	Percent of All Child Recipients	Child Recipients per 1,000 Children with Characteristic
Total	888,470	100.0	13.2
Age			
Under 3 years	62,090	6.9	4.7
3–5 years	120,990	13.6	9.5
6–12 years	384,380	43.3	13.0
13–17 years	269,420	30.4	13.5
18–21 years	51,560	5.8	n.a.
Sex			
Female	327,210	36.8	10.0
Male	561,260	63.2	16.3
Race			
White	331,660	37.3	6.2[a]
Black	306,090	34.5	28.6[a]
Hispanic	78,480	8.8	9.1[a]
Other	27,900	3.1	8.3[a]
Unknown	144,340	16.2	n.a.
Living Arrangements			
Parent's Household	709,980	79.9	n.a.
Another's Household	29,240	3.3	n.a.
Own Household[b]	137,588	15.5	n.a.
Medicaid Institution	11,670	1.3	n.a.
Family Structure			
One Parent	452,100	50.9	n.a.
Two Parents	263,240	29.6	n.a.
No Parents[c]	173,130	19.5	n.a.

n.a. = not available
a. The denominator includes children ages 0 to 19.
b. Living in "own household" refers to children whose parents' income is not considered in calculating benefit level. This includes children living with other relatives, in hospitals, nursing homes, residential schools, foster care, or independently.
c. These children reside independently, with other relatives or non-relatives, in institutions, or in foster care. Parents' income is not considered in calculating benefit level.
Source: Office of Supplemental Security Income Policy, "Children Receiving SSI," December 1994. The table is based on a 10-percent sample file of recipients with payments due January 1, 1995. Population figures are for 1993.

income is considered in eligibility calculations. This category includes children living with other relatives, in hospitals, nursing homes, residential schools, foster care, or independently. Less than 2 percent of children on SSI live in a medical facility where more than half of the cost of their care is covered by the Medicaid program.

(These children are only eligible for small monthly SSI payments.) Approximately half of children receiving SSI live with only one parent; another 30 percent live with both parents, with the remaining children in a living arrangement with no parents (e.g., in a residential care facility or foster care).

SSI child recipients can be categorized in a range of primary diagnostic or condition categories (Table 4.4).[14] More than 66 percent of SSI children were eligible by reason of a mental impairment, 23 percent with psychotic and neurotic disorders, and 43 percent with mental retardation. The next largest diagnostic category is diseases of the nervous system and sense organs which includes blind children. The distribution of children by diagnostic group varies with age, although for children over age three, mental retardation remains the largest category. For children under three, nervous system and sense organ conditions and congenital anomalies are the largest categories.

Many blind and disabled children remain on SSI for long periods of time. One study examined the first ten post-award years for persons awarded SSI between 1974 and 1982.[15] The authors found that over a third of all children remained on SSI continuously for the entire ten years and only 8 percent remained on SSI for less than a year. The length of stay varied across diagnostic groups with 46 percent of children with psychiatric diagnoses staying on for all ten years and 23 percent of children with respiratory conditions remaining on for the entire period. Slightly more than 8 percent of child SSI recipients died during the ten years after award. The authors project that the average SSI disability stay for children during their preretirement years (prior to age 65) is more than 25 years.

Related to these projected long recipiency periods is the number of current adult SSI recipients who first applied for SSI before the age of 18. In December 1994, there were 307,000 adult recipients who first applied for SSI before age 18. This represents 8 percent of current blind and disabled adult SSI recipients, and this figure will continue to grow as increased numbers of children receive SSI.

Expenditures

Total expenditures on SSI can be divided into three parts: federal SSI payments, supplemental state payments that are federally administered, and supplemental state payments that are state administered. Table 4.5 shows total payments for SSI in these categories from 1980 to 1993. As the table makes clear, total spending for children receiving SSI has increased rapidly over the last decade.[16] Total federal pay-

Table 4.4 NUMBER AND PERCENT OF CHILDREN RECEIVING SSI, BY
DIAGNOSTIC GROUP AND SELECTED AGE GROUPS, DECEMBER 1994

Diagnostic Group	Total	Under 3 years	13–17 years
	Number		
Total	888,470	62,090	269,420
Total with diagnosis	741,540	50,160	219,800
Infectious and parasitic	2,770	530	290
Neoplasms	12,060	750	2,690
Endocrine, nutritional, and metabolic	7,870	760	2,170
Mental disorders:			
Psychotic and neurotic disorders	171,240	3,540	59,350
Mental retardation	320,700	3,610	118,100
Diseases of the:			
Nervous system and sense organs	92,120	7,270	18,720
Circulatory system	5,250	1,400	770
Respiratory system	19,800	3,190	2,910
Digestive system	2,430	530	270
Musculoskeletal system and			
connective tissues	8,950	620	2,720
Congenital anomalies	33,340	9,430	3,440
Other	65,010	18,530	8,730

Diagnostic Group	Total	Under 3 years	13–17 years
	Percent		
Total with diagnosis	100.0	100.0	100.0
Infectious and parasitic diseases	0.4	1.1	0.1
Neoplasms	1.6	1.5	1.2
Endocrine, nutritional, and metabolic	1.1	1.5	1.0
Mental disorders:			
Psychotic and neurotic disorders	23.1	7.1	27.0
Mental retardation	43.2	7.2	53.7
Diseases of the:			
Nervous system and sense organs	12.4	14.5	8.5
Circulatory system	0.7	2.8	0.4
Respiratory system	2.7	6.4	1.3
Digestive system	0.3	1.1	0.1
Musculoskeletal system and			
connective tissues	1.2	1.2	1.2
Congenital anomalies	4.5	18.8	1.6
Other	8.8	36.9	3.8

Source: Office of Supplemental Security Income Policy, "Children Receiving SSI," December 1994. Based on a 10-percent sample of Social Security Administration records. Includes recipients with payments due January 1, 1995.

Table 4.5 ANNUALIZED SSI PAYMENTS TO BLIND AND DISABLED CHILDREN IN
CONSTANT DOLLARS, 1980 TO 1993 (IN MILLIONS OF 1993 DOLLARS)

Year	Total SSI Payments	Federal SSI Payments	Federally Administered State Supplementation	State Administered State Supplementation
1980	1,064.1	948.4	105.4	10.3
1981	1,067.0	960.8	96.3	9.9
1982	1,093.4	995.1	88.7	9.6
1983	1,166.3	1,074.6	81.6	10.1
1984	1,226.3	1,131.0	84.2	11.1
1985	1,299.8	1,197.6	90.5	11.7
1986	1,437.2	1,320.1	104.1	13.0
1987	1,455.6	1,331.5	110.9	13.3
1988	1,473.4	1,354.8	105.4	13.1
1989	1,495.2	1,375.5	106.3	13.4
1990	1,838.3	1,697.3	125.1	16.0
1991	2,511.1	2,355.5	136.6	19.0
1992	4,737.8	4,509.2	201.6	27.0
1993	4,283.9	4,081.7	176.5	25.8

Note: Federal and federally administered state payments are calculated by multiplying December caseload by average December payments for given year. State administered state payments are calculated using the percentage of total state administered payments relative to total federally administered state payments for the given year applied to the federally administered payments for blind and disabled children. All payments are annualized by multiplying the December payment figures by 12. Payments for 1991–1993 include retroactive payments to previously denied children under the *Zebley* decision. Figures are converted to 1993 dollars using the CPI-U index.
Source: Social Security Annual Statistical Supplement, 1980–1994 editions and Economic Report of the President, 1994.

ments were $948 million in 1980 (in 1993 dollars) and have increased to almost $4.3 billion in 1993. Part of the growth since 1991 is due to the inclusion of several years of retroactive payments to children who were previously denied SSI but were found eligible through redeterminations after the *Zebley* decision. The decrease in payments from 1992 to 1993 reflects a return toward current annual flows of payments for this year, since most of the previously denied cases have already been considered. While these retroactive payments exaggerate the growth in SSI expenditures in recent years, expenditures in constant dollars had almost doubled from 1980 to 1990, before eligibility changes were implemented.[17]

State supplementation payments have also increased over the past decade. Total state supplementation payments (in 1993 dollars) have increased from $116 million in 1980 to over $202 million in 1993.

Although the number of recipients was growing over this period, expenditures per child on SSI also grew over this time period. In 1993 dollars, total payments per child on SSI were $4,687 per year in 1980, $5,426 in 1990, and $5,587 in 1993.[18]

MEDICAID

The Medicaid program is among the most important sources of funding for health services for children with disabilities. The complexity of the program, including the numerous criteria for becoming eligible and the variety of services provided, makes it difficult to consider as a single program. The 1993 Medicaid Source Book prepared by the Congressional Research Service reports that Medicaid is often thought of as three different programs:[19]

- a basic health insurance plan for most of its beneficiaries;
- a financing program for long-term medical and social services for the frail elderly and disabled;
- a funding stream for programs (largely state-operated) for the developmentally disabled and mentally ill, both institutional and community-based.

These three different "program" distinctions are not entirely separate. For example, a child receiving services through a Medicaid-funded, community-based, mental retardation program may also receive acute care services, using Medicaid as a basic health insurance plan. Because of these overlaps, it is difficult to distinguish how many children with disabilities are receiving services under each program part, as well as to separate expenditures by program part.

Eligibility

There are at least four different ways children with disabilities can become eligible for Medicaid. These include: eligibility through SSI receipt, general eligibility provisions covering all children, medically needy programs, and special provisions for chronically ill or disabled children.

ELIGIBILITY THROUGH SSI

Most states are required by federal law to provide Medicaid eligibility to blind and disabled children receiving SSI. Thirty-one states and the District of Columbia provide Medicaid without separate application. Seven states opt to provide Medicaid to SSI recipients only if they make a separate application to the state agency that administers Medicaid. The states choosing this option are Alaska, Idaho, Kansas, Nebraska, Nevada, Oregon, and Utah.

Some states do not provide Medicaid to SSI recipients automatically. States are allowed to use more restrictive eligibility standards for Medicaid than for SSI if they were using those standards before the implementation of the SSI program. About 18 percent of all SSI recipients live in these states.[20] The twelve states using more restrictive standards in 1994, known as "section 209(b)" states, were: Connecticut, Hawaii, Illinois, Indiana, Minnesota, Missouri, New Hampshire, North Carolina, North Dakota, Ohio, Oklahoma, and Virginia. The more restrictive standards may include different definitions of disability or more restrictive income and asset eligibility criteria.

States using more restrictive eligibility requirements must allow applicants to deduct medical expenses from income before determining eligibility (called "spend down" provisions). In addition, states may optionally choose to provide Medicaid to persons not receiving federal SSI payments but who are receiving state supplemental SSI payments. As of January 1991, 34 states provided Medicaid automatically to persons receiving only supplemental state SSI payments.

States are required to continue Medicaid coverage for those who lose Medicaid under a variety of circumstances. The most important of these for children is the loss of SSI eligibility due to income increases, such as gaining social security benefits, when moving to adult status.

Because SSI eligibility insures Medicaid coverage for the majority of recipients, loss of eligibility for SSI, even because of a relatively small amount of additional earnings, can mean a major increase in costs for a family (through medical expenses). Although this is also a problem in other welfare programs, the SSI child with disabilities will more likely have higher costs and more persistent needs being met by Medicaid.

GENERAL ELIGIBILITY PROVISIONS FOR CHILDREN

Low-income families receiving cash assistance from the Aid to Families with Dependent Children (AFDC) program are also automatically eligible for Medicaid. AFDC is a program of cash assistance for poor families. As SSI is received by only a portion of all children with disabilities, it is likely that many poor children with some level of disability receive Medicaid through AFDC recipiency.

Over the last 10 years, Medicaid eligibility for pregnant women and children (unrelated to participation in cash assistance programs) has been greatly expanded. There are a variety of both mandatory expansions as well as optional expansions of the population to whom states may provide Medicaid. These are not specifically related to children with disabilities (there are only age and income requirements) but they also may help children who are not eligible for Medicaid through SSI.

Some of the major expansions in coverage required include: (1) all pregnant women, infants, and children under age 6 in families with income under 133 percent of poverty; (2) all children between age 6 and 19 born after September 30, 1983, in families with income under 100 percent of poverty; and (3) an additional 12 months of coverage for families who lose AFDC benefits due to increased earnings. In addition, states have the option of covering non-AFDC women and infants under age one with family income between 133 and 185 percent of poverty. As of July 1993, 34 states were using this option.

MEDICALLY NEEDY

The medically needy program may benefit families with children who have large medical expenditures but income too high to qualify for Medicaid through SSI or AFDC. Persons eligible for the medically needy program must meet the non-financial criteria for Medicaid, such as the disability criteria for SSI or family structure for AFDC. States may establish higher income or resource requirements for medically needy, up to 133 1/3 of the maximum payment under the state's AFDC program. They may also allow for "spend down": allowing deduction of medical expenses from income before assessing financial eligibility.

Medically needy programs are established at state option, although once established they must serve at least pregnant women and children. As of October 1993, 15 states did not have medically needy programs. States that do not have a medically needy program include: Alabama, Alaska, Arizona, Colorado, Delaware, Idaho, Indiana, Mississippi, Missouri, Nevada, New Mexico, Ohio, South Carolina, South Dakota, and Wyoming.[21]

SPECIAL PROVISIONS FOR CHRONICALLY ILL OR DISABLED CHILDREN:
TEFRA AND HCBS WAIVERS

Additional avenues of eligibility for children who are chronically ill or have a disability are available for children receiving care at home or in the community who would otherwise be in an institutional setting. Most children receiving care in an institutional setting are eligible for SSI (and therefore Medicaid) because, after 30 days, parental income is not considered in calculating eligibility; only the child's own financial resources are considered. When a child is living at home, however, parental income is considered available to that child when calculating eligibility. This can lead to a child being eligible for Medicaid if he or she is living in an institutional setting but not if he or she is living at home. The result is that some children may be in institutions in order to be eligible for Medicaid when they could receive care at home, care that is often less costly.

States have two options for extending Medicaid eligibility to children receiving care in the community or at home: the TEFRA option, and Home and Community-Based Services (HCBS) regular and model waivers.

Changes in TEFRA (Tax Equity and Fiscal Responsibility Act of 1982) allowed states the option of extending Medicaid to certain disabled children under 18 who are living at home and who would be eligible for SSI if they were living in a hospital, nursing facility, or intermediate care facility for the mentally retarded. This provision is sometimes called the Katie Beckett provision after the child whose case was used to publicize this need. The requirements for receiving Medicaid under this option include: (1) the child requires the level of care provided in an institution, (2) appropriate care can be provided to the child outside of an institution, and (3) the cost of care at home is no more than the cost in an institution. Children who have private insurance that covers the cost of institutional care are not eligible if their costs at home for Medicaid would be higher than in an institutional setting. States electing this option must cover all qualifying children. Currently, 18 states offer this provision.[22]

Medicaid also allows the states the option of applying for waivers to provide community-based services to individuals who would otherwise require (or be at risk of requiring) care in an institutional setting that could be covered by Medicaid. These waivers are called Home and Community-Based Services (HCBS) waivers or section 1915(c) waivers and can be used to provide services that would otherwise not be covered, although total Medicaid costs to individuals under a waiver cannot exceed the costs that Medicaid would pay for those individuals in institutional settings. Waivers can be used to target a subset of the state, such as certain geographic areas of a state or certain categories of beneficiaries. Eligibility depends on the specific waiver.

A variation of the 1915(c) waiver is called the "model" waiver. These waivers are used in the same way as the TEFRA option is used. For children who are receiving care at home but would be eligible for Medicaid if in an institutional setting, parental income is not considered in calculating Medicaid eligibility. The Health Care Financing Administration limits use of the model waiver to 200 individuals per waiver. Although the model waiver is similar to TEFRA, most states prefer the model waiver for two reasons. First, TEFRA requires provision of services to all who qualify, leading to uncertainty for a state in the total associated costs. Second, the model waiver allows flexibility in providing services usually not covered by Medicaid, while TEFRA limits services to those included in a state Medicaid program. Under a model waiver, states can provide potentially costly optional services to a limited set of individuals. Currently 14 states have model or regular HCBS waivers that serve children with special health care needs, including two waivers that serve only children with AIDS/ARC.

Administration

Each state operates its own Medicaid program through a state agency, usually the health department or welfare and social services department. The main functions of the state are to determine eligibility, process claims, certify providers, and assure the program is properly administered. States with automatic eligibility for Medicaid through SSI have the option of having eligibility determination carried out by the Social Security Administration. Most Medicaid claim payments are issued by the state directly to providers, not to beneficiaries.

At the federal level, Medicaid is administered by the Health Care Financing Administration (HCFA). Because states must comply with federal mandates, the state plan for Medicaid must be approved by HCFA. If the state wants to waive certain federal requirements, the state must apply for a waiver and have it approved by HCFA. HCFA also oversees state Medicaid programs' compliance with federal regulations.

Medicaid services are financed jointly by states and the federal government. The federal share of a state's Medicaid payments is known as the federal medical assistance percentage (FMAP). FMAPs are calculated annually based on a formula that gives higher federal matches to states with lower per capita incomes. The minimum

FMAP was 50 percent and the maximum was 83 percent in 1992. On average, the FMAP was 58 percent in 1992.

Benefits/Services

Medicaid provides a broad variety of services to children with disabilities. By federal mandate, a single set of services must be offered by all state Medicaid programs. There is also an additional set of services that states can offer at their option.[23]

The following services are mandatory: inpatient hospital services, outpatient hospital services, rural health clinic services, federally qualified health center services, other laboratory and x-ray services, nursing facility (NF) services for individuals 21 or older, early and periodic screening, diagnosis and treatment (EPSDT) services for individuals under age 21, family planning services, physicians' services, home health services for any individual entitled to NF care, nurse-midwife services, and services of certified nurse practitioners and certified family nurse practitioners.

There is also a set of services which state Medicaid programs may offer at their option. Optional services are as follows: podiatrists' services, optometrists' services, chiropractors' services, other practitioners' services, private duty nursing, clinic services, dental services, physical therapy, occupational therapy, speech, hearing and language disorder services, prescribed drugs, dentures, prosthetic devices, eyeglasses, diagnostic services, screening services, preventive services, rehabilitative services, intermediate care facilities (ICF) services for mentally retarded, inpatient psychiatric services for children under age 21, Christian Science nurses and sanatoria, nursing facilities (NF) for children under age 21, emergency hospital services, personal care services, transportation services, case management services, hospice services, and respiratory care services. The number of states providing some specific optional services are listed in Table 4.6.

Medicaid provides some benefits that differ from those covered by traditional medical insurance. These include the EPSDT program and non-medical HCBS waiver services. Under the EPSDT benefit, states must periodically provide general health screening, vision, hearing, and dental services for Medicaid recipients under age 21. States are required to provide each service type at appropriate intervals. Any services necessary to treat illnesses or conditions identified by screening that are covered (mandatory or optional) under federal Medicaid regulations must be provided by a state even if the services are not normally covered by the state's Medicaid program. Essentially, EPSDT

Table 4.6 NUMBER OF STATES PROVIDING OPTIONAL MEDICAID SERVICES,
DECEMBER 1993

Service	States Offering Services to Categorically Needy Only	States Offering Services to Categorically Needy and Medically Needy	Total
Psychologists	7	20	27
Physical Therapy	13	28	41
Speech Pathology/Audiology	16	31	47
Private Duty Nursing	8	20	28
Maternal & Child Health Clinic	14	27	41
Mental Health Clinic	14	25	39
MR/Day Treatment	2	9	11
Physical Therapy	13	28	41
Speech Disorders	14	26	40
Hearing Disorders	15	26	41
Language Disorders	13	24	37
Prescribed Drugs	16	35	51
Prosthetic Devices	18	33	51
Rehabilitative Services	13	32	45
ICF/MR	22	29	51
Inpatient Psychiatric (under 21)	13	28	41
TCM (under 21)	5	12	17
Respiratory Care Services	5	12	17
Transportation Services	15	36	51
NF Services (under 21)	20	31	51
Personal Care Services	11	21	32

Source: U.S. Department of Health and Human Services, Health Care Financing Administration, "Medicaid spDATA System: Characteristics of Medicaid State Programs," part 1, December 1993, Table 3-1.1.

requires states to cover the full range of mandatory and optional services for eligible Medicaid children. In fiscal year 1991, federal and state payments for EPSDT services totaled $356 million. This figure does not reflect all examinations received by children enrolled in Medicaid, as states may reimburse for some health supervision services that are not billed as EPSDT services.

Under the HCBS waiver program, additional services not regularly funded by Medicaid may be provided. The exact services depend on the specific state waiver. Some of the services available through waivers include case management, homemaker/home health aide services, personal care, adult day health services, habilitation services, respite care, supported employment services, minor home modifications, non-medical transportation, nutrition counseling, home-delivered meals, family therapy, psycho-social counseling, emergency response systems, medical supplies, and assistive devices. Some of these services are more commonly provided in waivers for the elderly than in waivers targeted at children with disabilities or persons with MR/DD.

Program Participation

The Health Care Financing Administration tracks state-level enrollee and expenditure information for the Medicaid program. In these administrative data, enrollees are usually categorized as aged, adults, blind/disabled, or children. Children categorized as blind and disabled are usually receiving Medicaid through SSI eligibility or SSI-related eligibility, or in long-term care paid for by Medicaid. However, some children with disabilities (depending on the definition used) are eligible for Medicaid by other routes, such as through the AFDC program or due to recent expansions in Medicaid eligibility for children. These children are most likely included in the "children" (not "blind and disabled") category and cannot be separated from other children in this category who *do not* have a disability. Because our attention has been limited to child Medicaid enrollees in the "blind and disabled" category, the participation and expenditure data reported underestimate Medicaid's service to all children with disabilities.[24]

Table 4.7 reports the number of blind and disabled child (under age 21) Medicaid enrollees by state in 1993.[25] Over 796,000 blind and disabled children in the United States were enrolled in Medicaid in 1993. This is compared to almost 38 million Medicaid enrollees in total and over 5 million blind and disabled enrollees in 1992.

The majority of these children qualified for Medicaid through SSI, since at the end of 1993 over 766,000 children were receiving SSI payments. While not all SSI recipients are automatically eligible for Medicaid, the majority are. Information reported to HCFA by states shows that 89 percent of children categorized as blind and disabled enrollees are also receiving cash assistance, usually through the SSI program. Most of the remaining 11 percent are in residential care paid for by Medicaid (such as inpatient psychiatric care or intermediate care facilities) or eligible through state medically needy programs.

Like SSI, Medicaid enrollment for children with disabilities varies across states, as shown in Table 4.7. Variation in enrollment per capita across states reflects differences in state incomes as well as individual state's Medicaid program's eligibility. For example, some states do not have a medically needy program. Also, states' use of Home and Community-Based Services waivers varies.

Table 4.7 BLIND AND DISABLED MEDICAID ENROLLEES UNDER AGE 21, BY STATE, 1993

State	Blind and Disabled Child Enrollees	Enrollees Per Thousand Residents Under 18	State Has Medically Needy Program	Waiver Exp. As % of Total Medicaid Payments
United States	796,279	11.9		1.9
Alabama	28,349	26.3	No	3.5
Alaska	661	3.5	No	0
Arkansas	20,571	32.4	Yes	0.3
California	70,748	8.2	Yes	1.1
Colorado	8,249	8.8	No	6.7
Connecticut	1,105	1.4	Yes	5.8
Delaware	2,633	15.0	No	4.2
District of Columbia	2,266	19.7	Yes	0
Florida	46,491	14.7	No	0.9
Georgia	27,051	14.7	Yes	1.7
Hawaii	662	2.2	Yes	3.0
Idaho	3,926	11.8	No	2.7
Illinois	33,791	11.0	Yes	2.6
Indiana	5,035	3.4	No	0
Iowa	7,586	10.3	Yes	0.2
Kansas	6,056	8.9	Yes	2.4
Kentucky	20,314	20.9	Yes	1.8
Louisiana	35,982	28.9	Yes	0.1
Maine	3,197	10.4	Yes	3.3
Maryland	10,809	8.7	Yes	2.7
Massachusetts	14,931	10.7	Yes	2.3
Michigan	32,068	12.8	Yes	1.8
Minnesota	7,022	5.7	Yes	4.9
Mississippi	27,000	35.6	No	0.2
Missouri	6,764	5.0	No	2.4
Montana	2,480	10.7	Yes	5.6

(continued)

Expenditures

As with participation, Medicaid expenditure data are collected from states by HCFA by categories of enrollee. Table 4.8 reports expenditures for all children under age 21 categorized as blind and disabled enrollees by state.[26] State and federal expenditures by Medicaid in 1993 for blind and disabled children totalled almost $6 billion. This compares to total Medicaid spending (for enrollees of all ages) of $125 billion. On average across states, federal spending was 58 percent of total Medicaid spending.

Table 4.7 BLIND AND DISABLED MEDICAID ENROLLEES UNDER AGE 21, BY
STATE, 1993 (continued)

State	Blind and Disabled Child Enrollees	Enrollees Per Thousand Residents Under 18	State Has Medically Needy Program	Waiver Exp. As % of Total Medicaid Payments
Nebraska	3,464	7.9	Yes	5.9
Nevada	2,071	5.9	No	2.0
New Hampshire	2,661	9.4	Yes	11.3
New Jersey	21,561	11.4	Yes	5.1
New Mexico	6,180	12.8	No	4.1
New York	74,140	16.6	Yes	0.1
North Carolina	4,781	2.8	Yes	1.7
North Dakota	954	5.5	Yes	8.0
Ohio	34,086	11.9	No	0.5
Oklahoma	8,859	10.2	Yes	1.4
Oregon	4,817	6.2	Yes	13.4
Pennsylvania	42,138	14.7	Yes	2.9
Rhode Island	n.a.	n.a.	Yes	3.4
South Carolina	14,050	14.8	No	2.4
South Dakota	2,763	13.3	No	7.1
Tennessee	30,064	23.7	Yes	0.5
Texas	54,711	10.6	Yes	0.3
Utah	2,732	4.1	Yes	6.1
Vermont	1,595	11.1	Yes	7.6
Virginia	14,870	9.4	Yes	2.6
Washington	10,331	7.4	Yes	5.8
West Virginia	11,310	26.1	Yes	3.2
Wisconsin	21,205	15.8	Yes	3.4
Wyoming	1,188	8.6	No	1.6

Note: Arizona and U.S. Territories not included. Data for Rhode Island are not available.
Source: Urban Institute calculations using HCFA forms 2064 and 2082. Enrollees include state reports of blind and disabled children under age 21.

Medicaid spending on blind and disabled children varies across
states. For most states, spending ranged from $5,000 to $10,000 per
enrollee. Spending variations across states are due to a number of
factors including differences in state Medicaid program eligibility and
optional Medicaid services provided.

The average Medicaid spending for blind and disabled children
(shown in Table 4.8) masks large variations in Medicaid spending
across children with different needs. For example, children in residential settings where Medicaid is paying all expenses, including
room and board, have high annual expenditures compared to children
who qualify for Medicaid but have little additional medical costs.
Expenditures for children under age 21 receiving services in inpatient

Table 4.8 MEDICAID EXPENDITURES FOR BLIND AND DISABLED CHILDREN
UNDER 21, BY STATE, 1993

State	Expenditures on Blind and Disabled Child Enrollees (in thousand $)	Expenditures per Blind and Disabled Child Enrollee	Expenditures per Resident Under Age 18
United States	$5,853,963	$ 7,352	$ 87.2
Alabama	112,307	3,962	104.3
Alaska	12,173	18,416	64.4
Arkansas	117,882	5,730	185.6
California	593,333	8,387	69.0
Colorado	71,370	8,652	76.1
Connecticut	30,652	27,740	39.6
Delaware	26,299	9,988	150.3
District of Columbia	21,827	9,633	189.8
Florida	230,693	4,962	72.8
Georgia	144,831	5,354	78.7
Hawaii	5,603	8,464	18.7
Idaho	25,954	6,611	77.9
Illinois	235,832	6,979	76.9
Indiana	93,053	18,481	63.3
Iowa	63,302	8,345	86.2
Kansas	63,548	10,493	92.9
Kentucky	105,757	5,206	108.9
Louisiana	289,084	8,034	232.6
Maine	39,472	12,346	128.6
Maryland	85,495	7,910	68.9
Massachusetts	188,874	12,650	135.6
Michigan	198,538	6,191	79.2
Minnesota	63,232	9,005	51.5
Mississippi	90,787	3,362	119.8
Missouri	58,958	8,716	43.3
Montana	27,580	11,121	118.9

(continued)

psychiatric facilities, intermediate care facilities for mental retardation (ICF/MR), or nursing and other facilities in 1993 are shown in
Table 4.9. More children are served in inpatient psychiatric facilities
(51,000) than in the other two categories combined (18,000). However,
per recipient, inpatient psychiatric services are less expensive
($20,000) than nursing facilities ($39,000) or ICF/MR services
($54,000). Differences in annual expenditures reflect variation in
length of stay and cost yearly. Annual expenditures for these services
far outweigh the average per child Medicaid spending for all blind
and disabled children in the United States of $7,350.

Table 4.8 MEDICAID EXPENDITURES FOR BLIND AND DISABLED CHILDREN
UNDER 21, BY STATE, 1993 *(continued)*

State	Expenditures on Blind and Disabled Child Enrollees (in thousand $)	Expenditures per Blind and Disabled Child Enrollee	Expenditures per Resident Under Age 18
Nebraska	21,623	6,242	49.3
Nevada	30,883	14,912	87.7
New Hampshire	7,518	2,825	26.6
New Jersey	214,672	9,956	113.2
New Mexico	47,319	7,657	98.4
New York	764,843	10,316	171.2
North Carolina	58,252	12,184	34.2
North Dakota	10,238	10,732	59.5
Ohio	208,821	6,126	73.0
Oklahoma	61,704	6,965	71.0
Oregon	26,922	5,589	34.4
Pennsylvania	344,046	8,165	119.8
South Carolina	84,755	6,032	89.0
South Dakota	23,724	8,586	114.1
Tennessee	110,574	3,678	87.1
Texas	429,739	7,855	82.9
Utah	27,048	9,901	40.7
Vermont	11,987	7,515	83.2
Virginia	76,354	5,135	48.1
Washington	79,015	7,648	56.7
West Virginia	52,172	4,613	120.2
Wisconsin	117,582	5,545	87.6
Wyoming	6,495	5,467	47.1

Note: Arizona, Rhode Island, and U.S. Territories not included.
Source: Data from Urban Institute calculations using HCFA forms 2064 and 2082.
Enrollees include state reports of blind and disabled children under age 21.

There is also significant variation in Medicaid expenditures among noninstitutionalized children. Table 4.10 shows the distribution of annual Medicaid expenditures per noninstitutionalized child on SSI in 1984 for three states, California, Georgia, and Michigan.[27] While average annual expenditures ranged from $1,300 to $2,100, median expenditures ranged from $240 to $410. The calculations are affected by a small percentage of Medicaid recipients who have very high annual expenditures. Recipients in the 95th percentile had expenditures more than 20 times higher than the median expense. Similar variation exists for noninstitutionalized Medicaid eligible blind and disabled children who are not receiving SSI.

Table 4.9 NUMBER OF AND EXPENDITURES ON MEDICAID RECIPIENTS UNDER
AGE 21, BY SELECTED SERVICE CATEGORY, 1993

Service Category	Recipients under Age 21	Expenditures (in thousands)	Expenditures per Recipient
Inpatient Psychiatric Services	51,470	$1,045,800	$20,319
Intermediate Care Facilities for			
Mental Retardation	12,526	681,210	54,384
Nursing Facilities	5,506	214,509	38,959
All Blind and Disabled Child			
Enrollees	796,279	5,853,963	7,352

Note: Data from Arizona, Rhode Island, and U.S. Territories not included. Data from
Urban Institute calculations using HCFA forms 2064 and 2082. Recipients are all
individuals under 21 actually receiving services.

Table 4.10 DISTRIBUTION OF ANNUAL MEDICAID EXPENDITURES PER
NONINSTITUTIONALIZED CHILD ELIGIBLE THROUGH SSI IN
CALIFORNIA, GEORGIA, AND MICHIGAN, 1984

	Expenditures per Noninstitutionalized Child Recipient Eligible through SSI		
	California	Georgia	Michigan
Average Annual Expenditure per			
Recipient	$2,104	$2,016	$1,255
Median Annual Expenditure per			
Recipient	396	411	239
Annual Expenditure per Recipient at			
25th Percentile	132	133	80
75th Percentile	1,347	1,697	788
90th Percentile	3,943	5,137	2,566
95th Percentile	7,678	9,374	4,754
Highest Annual Expenditure per			
Enrollee	536,085	83,595	216,128

Source: Marilyn Rymer Ellwood, "SSI-Related Disabled Children and Medicaid," prepared for the U.S. Department of Health and Human Services, Office of Family, Community, and Long-term Care Policy, Washington, D.C., June 1990, Table 10, p. 17. Data
are for recipients only.

Other sources of Medicaid spending for children with disabilities
include the TEFRA option and the HCBS waiver program. Table 4.11
shows the states that currently use the TEFRA option, the number of
children covered, and expenditures, where available. Overall 8,481
children were identified as receiving services through TEFRA. More
than half of these identified children live in Wisconsin or Minnesota.

Table 4.11 STATES USING MEDICAID TEFRA OPTION, 1994

State	Number of Recipients	Total Medicaid Expenditures for TEFRA Eligibles	Expenditures/ Recipient	Year of Data
Arkansas	227	n/a	n/a	1990
Delaware	620	$ 4,539,411	$ 7,322	1993
Georgia	84	n/a	n/a	1990
Idaho	483	3,404,891	7,049	1993
Massachusetts	210	4,181,372	19,911	1993
Maine	160	n/a	n/a	1990
Michigan	92	n/a	n/a	1990
Minnesota	3,226	25,796,988	6,510	1993
Mississippi	576	2,417,013	4,196	1993
Nebraska	9	n/a	n/a	1990
Nevada	141	2,759,950	19,574	1993
New Hampshire	16	n/a	n/a	1990
Pennsylvania	n/a	n/a	n/a	
Rhode Island	84	n/a	n/a	1990
South Dakota	2	n/a	n/a	1990
Vermont	28	n/a	n/a	1990
West Virginia	2	n/a	n/a	1990
Wisconsin	2,531	13,011,137	5,140	1991

Source: Sally Bachman and Brian Burwell, "Medicaid Home and Community Based Services for Children with Disabilities," technical memo to U.S. Department of Health and Human Services, Washington, D.C., October 1994. Data gathered by authors from personal contact with State Medicaid personnel.

Cost per recipient varied from $5,140 in Wisconsin to $19,911 in Massachusetts.

HCBS regular and model waiver programs served over 185,000 individuals in 1991 at a cost of $1.7 billion. HCBS spending in general has grown rapidly. Figure 4.3 shows the growth in total HCBS waiver program expenditures from 1982 to 1991, for persons of all ages. Table 4.12 lists states with HCBS model or regular waiver programs for children with special health care needs. These numbers exclude children served by waivers that are not limited to children (data on waivers serving developmentally disabled recipients, for example, are not reported by age). The HCBS waivers listed served 1,299 children, a small percentage of all persons served under this program. The total expenditure for children was over $13 million. Because each waiver provides different services and targets different populations, the cost per recipient varies widely from $1,106 to $116,266. An additional 1,782 children were served under two waivers specific to children with AIDS/ARC at a cost of over $2.5 million.[28]

Figure 4.3 FEDERAL AND STATE MEDICAID HOME AND COMMUNITY-BASED
WAIVER PROGRAM EXPENDITURES, FY 1982–1991

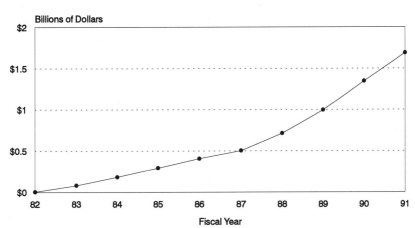

Source: Congressional Research Service analysis of HCFA Form 64 for fiscal years 1990–
1991; and Nancy Miller, "Medicaid 2176 Home and Community Based Care Waivers:
1982–89," paper presented at the 1990 annual meeting of the American Public Health
Association.

SPECIAL EDUCATION

Educational and support services for children with disabilities are
primarily administered and delivered to children by state and local
school systems. The main form of federal government educational
assistance is through the Individuals with Disabilities Education Act
(or IDEA).[29] The goal of the IDEA, as stated in its legislation, is "to
assure that all children with disabilities have available to them . . . a
free *appropriate* public education which emphasizes special education and related services designed to meet their unique needs, to
assure that the rights of children with disabilities and their parents
or guardians are protected, to assist states and localities to provide for the education of all children with disabilities, and to assess
and assure the effectiveness of efforts to educate children with disabilities."

Part B of the Act authorizes a state grant-in-aid program which
requires participating states to provide a free, appropriate public education to all children with disabilities in the state, regardless of the
nature or severity of their disability. IDEA also requires that (1) children receive their education in the least restrictive setting possible,

Table 4.12 MEDICAID HOME AND COMMUNITY-BASED SERVICES MODEL AND
REGULAR WAIVERS FOR CHILDREN WITH SPECIAL HEALTH CARE
NEEDS, 1990–91

State	Waiver Type	Waiver Recipients	Waiver Expenditures	Cost per Recipient
Total		1,299	$13,204,809	$12,331
Georgia	Model	24	739,918	30,830
Illinois	Model	185	343,725	1,858
Kentucky	Model	1	116,266	116,266
	Model	7	245,575	35,082
Maryland	Regular	173	4,028,648	23,287
	Model	9	977,625	108,625
New Mexico	Regular	79	1,207,719	15,288
New York	Model	180	199,126	1,106
	Model	181	·261,625	1,445
Ohio	Regular	200	1,124,993	5,625
Pennsylvania	Model	17	1,426,787	83,929
Rhode Island	Model	27	102,912	3,812
	Model	35	993,008	28,372
South Carolina	Model	1	15,001	15,001
Texas	Regular	160	675,757	4,223
Virginia	Model	20	493,666	24,683

Note: Table does not include children who receive services through state HCBS waivers
that are not targeted to children. It also does not include two state waivers in California
and New Jersey that provide services to 1,782 children with AIDS/ARC at a total expenditure of $2,501,964.

Source: Sally Bachman and Brian Burwell, "Medicaid Home and Community Based
Services for Children with Disabilities," technical memo to U.S. Department of Health
and Human Services, Washington, D.C., October 1994. Data abstracted from 1991 HCFA
Form 372 from each state.

(2) an Individualized Education Plan (IEP) be developed for each
child, and (3) the child be provided with any related services necessary to benefit from special education, including transportation,
speech therapy, and psychological therapy. Later amendments added
transition, assistive technology, rehabilitation counseling, and social
services to this list. Grant-in-aid funding is provided to support elementary and secondary education services for children between the
ages of 5 and 21. Amendments passed in 1986 added incentives for
states to serve all three- to five-year-olds with disabilities. By fiscal
year (FY) 1992, all states were required to provide a free and appropriate education to three- through five-year-old children with disabilities. Part H of IDEA established an early intervention program to
help states plan and implement a comprehensive program of early
intervention services for children from birth through two years of age.

One requirement of the early intervention program is that an Individualized Family Service Plan (IFSP) be developed for each child served.

Another federal program that has directly benefitted children with disabilities was funded under Chapter 1 of the Elementary and Secondary Education Act (ESEA), State Operated Programs (SOP). Chapter 1 (SOP) funds assisted states in the education of children with disabilities in state-operated and state-supported programs. In FY 1993, $126 million was appropriated for Chapter 1 (SOP) programs. Prior to the implementation of Part B, IDEA, Chapter 1 (SOP) was the only source of federal funding for students with disabilities. Beginning in 1992, the Congress decided to merge Chapter 1 (SOP) programs with those authorized under IDEA. Funding for Chapter 1 (SOP) decreased each year until FY 1995, when it was discontinued.[30]

Eligibility

Federal regulations establish categorical disability eligibility criteria for special education and related services. "Children with disabilities" are children evaluated as having mental retardation, hearing impairments including deafness, speech or language impairments, visual impairments including blindness, serious emotional disturbance, orthopedic impairments, autism, traumatic brain injury, other health impairments, specific learning disabilities, deaf-blindness, or multiple disabilities, and who because of those impairments need special education and related services. For children aged 3 through 5, states have the option of also including children who are experiencing developmental delays (in physical development, cognitive development, communication development, social or emotional development, or adaptive development) and who because of those developmental delays need special education and related services.

Federal guidelines on determination of eligibility for special education services are quite general. School districts vary a great deal in the terminology used for various disabilities, how children are assessed for placement, and how program types are defined. As one recent review of state and local operations found, "current practices in assessment, eligibility, and special education service delivery are shaped by multiple influences. These include federal legislation and regulation, state legislation and rules, professional standards, the current state of knowledge and technology, individual decisions made by practitioners, community values, availability of resources and funding, training of personnel, parental involvement in educational programs, and numerous other influences."[31]

Administration

The federal-level agency responsible for special education is the Office of Special Education and Rehabilitative Services (OSERS) within the U.S. Department of Education. At the state level, special education programs are administered by a state agency designated by the governor. This agency may be located in any of several state government departments but is most often found in state departments of education or public instruction.

Children receiving special education are given any related services outlined in their IEP. These are developed for each child by a multidisciplinary team of professionals. It is widely believed that in many localities these teams are under heavy pressure to minimize the number and intensity of related services because of their high cost. In other words, special education and related services are rationed. Cross-program linkages involving schools may be difficult to forge. Some schools may be reluctant to enter into collaborative agreements with other service providers in the community for fear that they will be held responsible for providing high cost services to children identified by these other providers.

There is also an incentive for school officials to place some slower-learning students in special education so that they are netted out of the testing population (in order to maximize test scores for the school or school district).[32] Also some parents may want their child to receive special education services to help them prove eligibility in their application for SSI benefits (the standards for the latter are much more rigorous). Similarly, there is anecdotal evidence that some parents may be reluctant to have their children switched from a high-intensity service environment (to a less restrictive setting) for fear of jeopardizing their SSI benefits.

Benefits/Services

The basic benefit provided to eligible children with disabilities is "a free appropriate public education." IDEA defines special education as "specially designed instruction, at no cost to parents or guardians, to meet the unique needs of a child with a disability, including classroom instruction, instruction in physical education, home instruction, and instruction in hospitals and institutions." In addition, children receive related services which are defined as "transportation, and such developmental, corrective, and other supportive services . . . as may be required to assist a child with a disability to benefit from special education, . . . " including speech pathology and audiology, psychological services, physical and occupational therapy, recreation, counseling, medical services (for diagnostic and evaluation purposes), and early identification and assessment of disabling conditions in children.

Since the passage of IDEA, there have been problems with the identification and assessment of students with mild to moderate disabilities.[33] Some assessment tools have been unable to differentiate between specific learning disabilities, serious emotional disturbance, and mild mental retardation. In addition, some research has found few differences between students with specific learning disabilities and unidentified students with learning or behavioral problems.

Program Participation

In 1992–93, approximately 5.2 million children from birth through age 21 were served under IDEA and Chapter 1 (SOP), an increase of 3.7 percent from the previous year (see Table 4.13). Among these children were 460,000 preschoolers (9 percent more than were served in 1991–92). Over half (51.1 percent) of the 4.6 million students between the age of 6 through 21 were identified as having a specific learning disability (see Table 4.14).[34] Another 22 percent had a speech or language impairment, 12 percent were classified with mental retardation, and 9 percent had a serious emotional disturbance. The disability distribution of special education students has not only been changing over time (see Figure 4.4), but also varies by program type (see Table 4.15). Children in self-contained classrooms, for example, are much more likely to be mentally retarded than special education students taken as a whole. Disability distribution patterns have also been found to vary by students' race and ethnicity.[35]

Expenditures

Federal IDEA, Part B State Grant Program funds are distributed to states according to the total number of students with disabilities who receive special education and related services. A count of the number of such students in the state (as of December 1st of the previous fiscal year) is submitted annually by state educational agencies (SEAs) to the Office of Special Education Programs. In FY 1993, $2.053 billion

Table 4.13 SPECIAL EDUCATION STUDENTS SERVED UNDER PART B AND
CHAPTER 1 (SOP): NUMBER AND PERCENTAGE CHANGE,
SCHOOL YEARS 1976–77 THROUGH 1992–93

School Year	Percent Change in Total Number Served from Previous Year	Total Served	Part B	Chapter 1 (SOP)
1976–77	—	3,708,588	3,484,756	223,832
1977–78	1.8	3,777,286	3,554,554	222,732
1978–79	3.8	3,919,073	3,693,593	225,480
1979–80	3.0	4,036,219	3,802,475	233,744
1980–81	3.5	4,177,689	3,933,981	243,708
1981–82	1.3	4,233,282	3,990,346	242,936
1982–83	1.5	4,298,327	4,052,595	245,732
1983–84	1.0	4,341,399	4,094,108	247,291
1984–85	0.5	4,363,031	4,113,312	249,719
1985–86	0.2	4,370,244	4,121,104	249,140
1986–87	1.2	4,421,601	4,166,692	254,909
1987–88	1.4	4,485,702	4,226,504	259,198
1988–89	1.8	4,568,063	4,305,690	262,373
1989–90	2.4	4,675,619	4,411,681	263,938
1990–91	2.8	4,807,441	4,547,368	260,073
1991–92	3.7	4,986,075	4,714,119	271,956
1992–93	3.7	5,170,242	4,893,865	276,377

Source: U.S. Department of Education, *To Assure the Free Appropriate Public Education of All Children with Disabilities, Sixteenth Annual Report to Congress on the Implementation of The Individuals with Disabilities Education Act,* Washington, D.C., 1994.

was distributed to states for special education and related services under IDEA, Part B and the average allocation per child was $411 (see Table 4.16). Programs funded under Chapter 1 (SOP) that assist in the education of children with disabilities in state-operated or state-supported programs received an average per-pupil allocation of $432. Total federal spending for Chapter 1 (SOP) in FY 1993 was $126 million.[36]

Although examining federal outlays for special education is a fairly straightforward matter, assessing the total costs of special education is much more complicated. One common approach is to compare per-pupil expenditures for special education to per-pupil expenditures for regular education. This comparison fails to account for the fact that many special education students spend part (if not most) of their day in a regular education classroom. If a student spends part of his or her day in a resource room, for example, one way of calculating the cost is to add the per-pupil cost of the resource room to the per-pupil

Table 4.14 DISABILITY OF STUDENTS AGE 6 THROUGH 21 SERVED UNDER
PART B AND CHAPTER 1 (SOP): NUMBER AND PERCENTAGE,
SCHOOL YEAR 1992–93

	Part B		Chapter 1 (SOP)		Total	
Disability	Number	Percent[a]	Number	Percent[a]	Number	Percent[a]
Specific learning disabilities	2,333,571	52.4	35,814	19.7	2,369,385	51.1
Speech or language impairments	990,718	22.2	9,436	5.2	1,000,154	21.6
Mental retardation	484,871	10.9	48,844	26.9	533,715	11.5
Serious emotional disturbance	368,545	8.3	34,123	18.8	402,668	8.7
Multiple disabilities	86,179	1.9	17,036	9.4	103,215	2.2
Hearing impairments	43,707	1.0	17,189	9.5	60,896	1.3
Orthopedic impairments	46,498	1.0	6,423	3.5	52,921	1.1
Other health impairments	63,982	1.4	2,072	1.1	66,054	1.4
Visual impairments	18,129	0.4	5,682	3.1	23,811	0.5
Autism	12,238	0.3	3,289	1.8	15,527	0.3
Deaf-blindness[b]	773	0.0	652	0.4	1,425	0.0
Traumatic brain injury	2,906	0.1	997	0.5	3,903	0.1
All disabilities	4,452,117	100.0	181,557	100.0	4,633,674	100.0

a. Percentages sum within columns.
b. 8,404 persons between the ages of birth to 21 have been identified by coordinators
of the State and Multi-State Services for Children with Deaf-Blindness.
Source: U.S. Department of Education, *To Assure the Free Appropriate Public Education of All Children with Disabilities*, Sixteenth Annual Report to Congress on the
Implementation of The Individuals with Disabilities Education Act, Washington, D.C.,
1994.

cost of regular education. Alternatively, one might pro-rate the per-
pupil resource room and regular education costs according to how
much time a given student spends in each setting. Some researchers
have distinguished between *supplemental* services (the costs for
which are completely in excess of expenditures for regular education)
and *replacement* services and costs (which are not in excess of those
for regular education).

One review of the costs of special education finds that while special
education expenditures represent a growing share of overall elementary and secondary school spending, this growth is due to the increas-

Figure 4.4 PERCENTAGE OF CHILDREN AGE 6–21 SERVED UNDER IDEA, PART B
BY DISABILITY: SCHOOL YEARS 1976–77 THROUGH 1993–1994

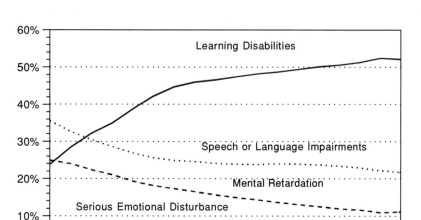

School Year

Source: U.S. Department of Education, Office of Special Education Programs, Data
Analysis Systems.

ing number of students served and the changing composition of students' needs rather than a real increase over time in the cost of serving a given student with similar needs.[37] The main study reviewed reports that total average per-pupil special education costs are about $6,335 (in 1985–86 dollars), or about 2.3 times the corresponding cost for regular education (see Table 4.17).[38] The cost estimates vary considerably by educational setting with resource rooms costing the least and self-contained classrooms and residential schools costing the most. This variation among different settings reflects both different types of conditions presented by special education students and differences in the actual cost of serving students with similar conditions (Table 4.18).

It is not clear whether more precise estimates of the costs of special education (at least at the national level) will be developed in the future. The collection of the type of detailed, comparable data needed from local school districts to support reliable national estimates of the costs of special education would probably require a level of administrative and accounting consistency (across school districts) that is not currently planned. As a report by the National Association of

Table 4.15 PERCENTAGE DISTRIBUTION OF SPECIAL EDUCATION STUDENTS
ENROLLED BY DISABILITY AND PROGRAM TYPE, SCHOOL YEAR
1985–86

Disability	Total	Preschool	Self-contained	Resource Room
Speech or language impairments	25%	19%	2%	36%
Mental retardation	14%	25%	42%	4%
Orthopedic impairments	1%	6%	2%	a/
Multiple disabilities	2%	10%	6%	a/
Specific learning disabilities	45%	7%	25%	52%
Serious emotional disturbance	7%	9%	18%	4%
Deafness	a/	1%	2%	a/
Deaf-blindness	a/	a/	a/	a/
Hearing impairments	1%	3%	2%	2%
Other health impairments	a/	2%	a/	a/
Autism	a/	1%	1%	a/
Visual impairments	1%	3%	a/	1%
Noncategorical	3%	14%	a/	a/
All conditions	100%	100%	100%	100%

a/ Less than 1 percent.
Source: Stephen Chaikind, Louis C. Danielson, and Marsha L. Brauen, "What Do We
Know About the Costs of Special Education? A Selected Review," The Journal of Special
Education, Vol. 26, No. 4, 1993, drawing on data reported in Mary T. Moore, E. William
Strang, Myron Schwartz, and Mark Braddock, Patterns in Special Education Service
Delivery and Cost (U.S. Department of Education Contract No. 300-84-0257), Decision
Resources Corporation, Washington, D.C., December 1988.

State Directors of Special Education concluded, "the autonomy that
states and local school districts have over their budget and accounting
systems makes it virtually impossible to collect data that are comparable and useful when aggregated at a national level. Consequently, it
has been suggested that reliable generalizations about the cost of special education cannot be made until there is a uniform basis for describing them. In the future, any proposed system for evaluating special education costs will have to take into consideration the diversity
of local conditions influencing the market price of educational goods
and services, and the ways in which local communities govern their
educational system."[39]

PART H EARLY INTERVENTION SERVICES

Part H of IDEA supports early intervention services for infants and
toddlers with disabilities through a coordinated system of family-

Table 4.16 IDEA, PART B STATE GRANT PROGRAM: FUNDS APPROPRIATED,
FISCAL YEARS 1977–93

Appropriation Year	IDEA, Part B State Grants	Percent Change	Per-Child Allocation[a]	Percent Change
1977	$ 251,770,000	—	$ 71	—
1978	566,030,000	125	156	120
1979	804,000,000	42	215	38
1980	874,190,000	9	227	6
1981	874,500,000	0	219	−4
1982	931,008,000	6	230	5
1983	1,017,900,000	9	248	8
1984	1,068,875,000	5	258	4
1985	1,135,145,000	6	272	5
1986	1,163,282,000	2	279	3
1987	1,338,000,000	15	316	13
1988	1,431,737,000	7	332	5
1989	1,475,449,000	3	336	1
1990	1,542,610,000	5	343	2
1991	1,854,186,000	20	400	17
1992	1,976,095,000	7	410	3
1993	2,052,730,000	4	411	0

a. Technical adjustments to the per-child allocation have been made to more accurately reflect the actual distribution of per-child funds to the states. These data do not match those included in previous annual reports.
Source: U.S. Department of Education, *To Assure the Free Appropriate Public Education of All Children with Disabilities, Sixteenth Annual Report to Congress on the Implementation of The Individuals with Disabilities Education Act*, Washington, D.C., 1994.

centered community-based services. By identifying very young children who may benefit from Part H services, the program may minimize (if not prevent) a later need for special education or institutionalization. Part H was enacted in 1986 when the federal government provided states with a five-year discretionary-formula grant for planning and implementation activities. From the beginning, the Part H Early Intervention amendment was cast as a systems change initiative, using many existing programs, agencies, and funding sources to serve the developmental needs of infants and toddlers, and their families. By law, state Part H systems are required to have the following components:[40]

• a definition of the term "developmentally delayed" for determining the eligibility of infants and toddlers for services under the state's program;

Table 4.17 SUMMARY OF SPECIAL EDUCATION COST INFORMATION: TOTAL AND BY PROGRAM TYPE, SCHOOL YEAR 1985–86, ALL DISABILITIES (IN CURRENT YEAR DOLLARS)

Type of Expenditure	All Programs	Preschool	Self-contained	Resource Room	Residential
Average total per-pupil expenditures for special education	$3,649	$4,750	$5,566	$2,463	$29,108
Average total per-pupil expenditures for regular education	$2,780	$2,780	$2,780	$2,780	$2,780
Average total per-pupil expenditures for portion of regular education services provided to special education students when in regular education environment	$2,686	$973	$1,347	$2,780	$389
Combined average total per-pupil expenditures for special and regular education	$6,335	$5,723	$6,913	$5,243	$29,497
Excess per-pupil cost for special education students	$3,555	$2,943	$4,133	$2,463	$26,717

Source: Stephen Chaikind, Louis C. Danielson, and Marsha L. Brauen, "What Do We Know About the Costs of Special Education? A Selected Review," The Journal of Special Education, Vol. 26, No. 4, 1993, drawing on data reported in Mary T. Moore, E. William Strang, Myron Schwartz, and Mark Braddock, Patterns in Special Education Service Delivery and Cost (U.S. Department of Education Contract No. 300-84-0257), Decision Resources Corporation, Washington, D.C., December 1988.

Table 4.18 AVERAGE PER-PUPIL SPECIAL EDUCATION EXPENDITURES, BY DISABILITY AND MAJOR PROGRAM TYPE, SCHOOL YEAR 1985–86 (IN CURRENT YEAR DOLLARS)

Disability	Preschool	Self-contained	Resource Room	Resource and Self-contained	Resource, Self-contained, Home/hospital, and Residential
Speech or language impairments	$3,062	$ 7,140	$ 647	$ 737	$ 737
Mental retardation	$3,983	$ 4,754	$2,290	$ 4,643	$ 4,615
Orthopedic impairments	$4,702	$ 5,248	$3,999	$ 5,132	$ 4,812
Multiple disabilities	$5,400	$ 6,878	NA	$ 6,878	$ 7,232
Specific learning disabilities	$3,708	$ 3,083	$1,643	$ 2,013	$ 2,058
Serious emotional disturbance	$4,297	$ 4,857	$2,620	$ 4,510	$ 5,300
Deafness	$5,771	$ 7,988	NA	$ 7,988	$10,947
Deaf-blindness	NA	$20,416	NA	$20,416	$31,416
Hearing impairments	$4,583	$ 6,058	$3,372	$ 4,594	$ 4,733
Other health impairments	$3,243	$ 4,782	NA	$ 4,782	$ 3,024
Autism	$6,265	$ 7,582	NA	$ 7,582	$17,236
Visual impairments	$4,068	$ 6,181	$3,395	$ 3,850	$ 5,317
Noncategorical	$3,686	$ 3,684	$1,731	$ 2,467	$ 2,467
Average per-pupil expenditures for instructional programs	$3,437	$ 4,233	$1,325	NA	NA
Average per-pupil expenditures for special education	$4,750	$ 5,566	$2,463	NA	NA

Source: Stephen Chaikind, Louis C. Danielson, and Marsha L. Brauen, "What Do We Know About the Costs of Special Education? A Selected Review," The Journal of Special Education, Vol. 26, No. 4, 1993, drawing on data reported in Mary T. Moore, E. William Strang, Myron Schwartz, and Mark Braddock, Patterns in Special Education Service Delivery and Cost (U.S. Department of Education Contract No. 300-84-0257), Decision Resources Corporation, Washington, D.C., December 1988.

- timetables for ensuring that appropriate early intervention services will be available to all infants and toddlers with disabilities in the state before the fifth year of the state's official participation in this federal program (allowing up to two waiver years);
- timely, comprehensive, multidisciplinary evaluations of the service needs of infants and toddlers with disabilities and their families;
- an "individualized family services plan" (IFSP) for each eligible infant and toddler with a disability in need of services, including timely procedures for making referrals to appropriate service providers;
- a comprehensive "child find" system to locate infants and toddlers with disabilities in need of services, including timely procedures for making referrals to appropriate service providers;
- a public awareness program focusing on early identification of infants and toddlers with disabilities;
- a central directory of early intervention services, resources, and expertise as well as research and demonstration projects being conducted within the state;
- a comprehensive personnel development system;
- a designated lead state agency to administer the program and serve as the fixed point of accountability;
- interagency agreements addressing components necessary to ensure effective cooperation and coordination, including provisions for dispute resolution and assignment of financial responsibility;
- a policy governing contracting or making other arrangements with providers of early intervention services;
- policies and procedures relating to financial matters, including a procedure for insuring the timely delivery of services and prompt reimbursement of funds used under Part H;
- procedural safeguards with respect to the provision of early intervention services;
- a data collection and management system for serving infants and toddlers with disabilities and their families; and
- procedures for resolving complaints.

By the fifth and final planning year, states were required to demonstrate that all components of the statewide system were in place, and that all eligible infants, toddlers, and families had access and were entitled to the full array of Part H services.

The latest annual report to Congress on the implementation of IDEA describes states' progress in establishing Part H services as follows:

Fragmentation, duplication, and overlap in services—initially identified soon after enactment of P.L. 99-457 [Part H of IDEA] as barriers to the development of a coordinated, interagency system—continue to be pronounced. A 50-state survey completed in 1992 by the Carolina Policy Studies Program (CPSP) indicated that as many as 44 sources of funding were found in all the States. So many sources impedes development of efficient funding mechanisms. CPSP discovered that 25 laws and programs addressed, in some fashion, the same target population. Thus, policymakers face difficulty in establishing eligibility, predicting the range of needed services, estimating costs for such services, and identifying the appropriate children to provide intervention. These difficulties have contributed to the States' reluctance to add the at-risk population to the group of eligible children, because the service and fiscal implications remain too uncertain.

Eligibility

Federal legislation requires that children eligible for Part H services include those who manifest developmental delays and children diagnosed with physical or mental conditions likely to cause a delay. States also have the option to serve infants and toddlers who are medically and/or environmentally *at risk* for substantial delay in the absence of early intervention services. Each jurisdiction must define more precisely the three potentially eligible groups of children (developmentally delayed, diagnosed condition with probability of delay, and at-risk for delay). As a result, the population of children eligible for Part H services differs considerably from one state to the next.

Administration

At the federal level, the Part H program is overseen by the Office of Special Education Programs (OSEP) within the U.S. Department of Education. At the state level, any of several agencies may be designated as the "lead agency" for Part H services. As of 1992, 19 states (including 2 with joint lead agencies) assigned their education agency to be the lead agency and 22 assigned their health agency to be the lead agency (in most of these the Title V Program serves as the Part H lead agency). The remaining states designated other types of agencies (Developmental Disabilities, Human Resources, or Services, Social Services, and Welfare) to be the lead Part H services agency.

Benefits/Services

Children who are identified and referred to the Part H system for evaluation and assessment are first assigned a family services coordinator.[41] A multi-disciplinary team then identifies the child's abilities and needs, the family's concerns, needs, and resources as they relate to the child's development, and the type and scope of services needed to meet the child's needs. With the family's full participation, an Individual Family Service Plan (IFSP) is developed. In addition to specific goals, the IFSP outlines the criteria, methods, and schedule for evaluating how established goals are being met, as well as the specific services needed and funding sources for these services. An important goal is to enhance the capabilities of the family in caring for and making decisions about the child.

Except where state law allows for family payments on a sliding fee scale, Early Intervention services must be delivered under public supervision at no cost to the family. Among the types of services that can be included in the IFSP are: audiology; family training, counseling, and home visits; health services needed to enable the child to benefit from early intervention; diagnostics/evaluation medical services; social work services; speech language pathology; physical therapy; case management; nursing services; nutrition services; occupational therapy; psychological services; special instruction; and transportation.

The most commonly provided services (as reported by states to the Department of Education) are: special instruction, speech/language pathology, social work, occupational therapy, and physical therapy. Based on limited data, it appears that the most common service site is the home (with 34 percent of services being delivered there), followed by early intervention classrooms (33 percent), and outpatient centers (29 percent).[42]

Program Participation

States have only just fully implemented the Part H program. As a result, data on the number of infants and toddlers served and the types of services they have received are incomplete. The latest data (reported in the Department of Education's 1994 report to Congress) reflect the number of infants and toddlers receiving early intervention services under Chapter 1 (SOP) and "other programs" on December 1, 1992. On that date, states estimate that they provided early intervention services to 76,397 children under the Chapter 1 (SOP) program and another 66,943 through other programs. Note that this presents a snapshot in time of the number of infants and toddlers being served. The annual numbers being served are larger. It is expected that as states gain more experience with Part H program requirements, greater consistency in how eligibility is defined and how data are collected will yield more reliable data.

Expenditures

There are four major sources of funds for Part H planning and service delivery: Part H federal funds, other federal funds such as Medicaid and Chapter 1, private insurance coverage, and state appropriations. Federal Part H funds are primarily intended for planning, implementation, and expansion activities and are not supposed to cover the operating costs of state programs. Other federal funding sources, however, do cover early intervention services. These include Medicaid, Chapter 1, Maternal and Child Health Block Grants, Child Care Block Grants, and Developmental Disabilities Basic State Grants. These sources, along with private insurance payments,[43] cover a substantial share of state and local expenditures for Part H early intervention services. Depending on how states structure their Medicaid program, federal Medicaid dollars can be used to cover between 50 and 80 percent of the costs of certain Part H services for many eligible infants and toddlers.[44]

As with special education, information on federal-level appropriations for Part H Early Intervention programs is readily available. Congress appropriated $175 million in Part H funds for states in FY 1992 and $213.3 million in FY 1993. A 1991 report by the National Conference on State Legislatures notes that state appropriations for early intervention services vary considerably from one state to another, ranging "from $20 million in Pennsylvania, $100,000 in Indiana, to nothing in Maryland and Mississippi."[45] Analyses of data submitted by states for 1989–90 suggest that total Part H expenditures were financed as follows: 13 percent federal Part H allocations, 10 percent Chapter 1 (SOP), 13 percent federal Medicaid, 32 percent other federal funds (including Maternal and Child Health and Child Care block grants), 20 percent state Part H appropriations, 6 percent state Medicaid funds, and 6 percent private insurance and other sources.[46] These estimates should be interpreted with caution for several reasons. As with most national estimates of programs administered at the state and local levels, national figures mask the very high level of diversity across states and local jurisdictions. Also, in 1989–90, states had not fully implemented their Part H programs and so current funding patterns differ. In particular, the 32 percent from other federal sources probably overestimates current Part H funding patterns. Finally, funding under Chapter 1 (SOP) has gradually been shifted to IDEA, so these two sources are best considered jointly.

The latest annual report to Congress on the implementation of IDEA confirms how little is known about actual aggregate or per-child costs of Part H services:

> A study by the National Early Childhood Technical Assistance System (NEC*TAS) underscored how hard it is to calculate per child and aggregate costs of Part H services. Many factors complicate the task of projecting costs, such as State eligibility definitions, estimating Part H population size, overlap with existing State and local fiscal commitment to early intervention services, participation rates, location of services, and the range of services that may be needed by a child or family. The four states that had already attempted completed cost studies— California, Florida, Maryland, and Virginia—reported per child costs for children with developmental delays (not for children classified as at-risk) ranging from $4,312 (Virginia) to $6,090 (Maryland).[47]
>
> But the range of per child costs is best illustrated by a detailed analysis in the California study, which attempted to provide cost figures for children with fairly specific developmental profiles. Annual costs ranged from $659 for a child with mild speech delays of unknown etiology diagnosed at 18 months of age, to $15,060 for a child of between 2 and 3 years who had been identified at 6 months of age with severe cerebral palsy and who also had motor functioning, feeding, and speech impairments.

Several state-level studies (including the Perry Preschool Study) suggest that for each dollar invested in early intervention services, states may save as much as three to seven dollars in special education and institutionalization costs.[48]

MATERNAL AND CHILD HEALTH BLOCK GRANTS

The Maternal and Child Health (MCH) Services Block Grant, authorized under Title V of the Social Security Act, consists of a program of formula grants to states (85 percent of the Block Grant) and two federal discretionary grant programs (Special Projects of Regional and National Significance and the Community Integrated Services System). In 1981 federal funding for the Title V MCH program was reduced by over 20 percent and six categorical programs were folded into the existing Title V Maternal and Child Health Services (MCH) and Children with Special Health Care Needs (CSHCN) programs. The programs absorbed into the MCH Services Block Grant were the SSI Disabled Children's program and the Public Health Service Act programs related to lead poisoning, genetic diseases, hemophilia, Sudden Infant Death Syndrome (SIDS), and adolescent pregnancy.

The goal of the MCH Block Grant program is to improve the health of *all* mothers and children consistent with state and national health objectives. Within federal guidelines, states are given considerable discretion to determine program needs, set priorities, and allocate funds. As a result, state programs funded under MCH block grants vary widely in size, organization, and scope of activities.

State Title V programs lay the foundation needed for effective planning and implementation of maternal and child health services for the population as a whole through state-wide needs assessments, the setting of standards, monitoring of services, and the provision of training and technical assistance. In addition, state Title V programs support the availability and accessibility of community health and family support services through direct services and/or through grants, contracts, or reimbursement to private and public sector providers. Families whose children experience selected chronic illness and disability are assisted through the program in obtaining the complex array of services they require.

Many of the activities states are authorized to subsidize with MCH block grant funds are preventative in nature, such as activities designed to reduce infant mortality and the incidence of preventable diseases.[49] In addition, the statute allows states to use MCH block grant funds to:

- provide rehabilitation services for individuals under the age of 16 who are blind or disabled or receiving Supplemental Security Income benefits (to the extent that these are not covered by Medicaid);
- provide and promote family-centered, community-based, coordinated care, particularly for children with special health care needs; and
- facilitate the development of community-based service systems for children with special health care needs and their families.

To achieve these ends, state MCH programs provide supportive linkages with, and in some cases administer, other programs serving children with special health care needs. These programs include Part H Early Intervention services, Early and Periodic Screening, Diagnosis,

and Treatment (EPSDT) services, and the Supplemental Feeding Program for Women, Infants, and Children (WIC).
Title V funds may not be used for:

* inpatient services other than those provided to children with special health care needs or to high risk pregnant women and infants and other inpatient services approved by the Secretary of HHS;
* cash payments to recipients for health care services;
* the purchase and improvement of land, construction, or permanent improvement of buildings or purchase of major medical equipment (unless a Secretarial waiver is obtained);
* matching other federal grants;
* providing funds for research or training to any entity other than a public or private nonprofit organization; or
* purchasing items or services furnished by practitioners who are excluded from participation in Medicare or state health care programs.

Eligibility

States establish their own financial and medical eligibility criteria. As a result, each state has its own unique set of criteria.[50]

Administration

At the federal level, Title V is administered by the Maternal and Child Health Bureau, within the Health Resources and Services Administration, U.S. Public Health Service. State Title V programs are administered by state health agencies, although in 10 states the Children with Special Health Care Needs (CSHCN) program is located in another state agency or university, maintaining arrangements established prior to 1967.[51]

Benefits/Services

The vast majority of state Title V MCH Block Grant funding is devoted to core public health functions including: (1) infrastructure and capacity building (such as needs assessment, planning, coordination, quality assurance, and standards development), and (2) population-based services (such as newborn screenings, immunization, lead poisoning prevention, outreach, and public education). In addition, MCH programs support enabling services such as case management, health education, transportation, translation, and nutrition. Finally, MCH funds are also used for direct personal health services, although these account for no more than 25 percent of state MCH program spending.

In the first quarter of 1993, the Maternal and Child Health Policy Research Center surveyed the directors of state CSHCN programs.[52] The purpose of the survey was to collect baseline data in order to track states' progress toward the Year 2000 system development goals. Preliminary results from the draft survey are listed below.[53]

SERVICES PROVIDED OR SUPPORTED BY TITLE V CSHCN PROGRAMS

- Almost all offer initial assessments, service planning, periodic follow-up, outpatient and inpatient specialty services, ancillary therapies, and coordination of care to at least some of their clients;
- Between 70–90 percent deliver or pay for advocacy and education, transportation, home health services, and family support and counseling.[54]

PLANNING AND DESIGN OF SERVICE SYSTEMS FOR CHILDREN WITH SPECIAL HEALTH NEEDS

- All CSHCN programs have achieved some progress in this area; 57 percent (29 states) report they have made much progress and 43 percent (22 states) report some progress;
- More than two-thirds of all states cite a great deal of progress in collaborating with Medicaid, the SSI program, and other state health programs;
- One-half of all states report a high level of collaborative effort with parent groups, provider groups, special education services, and developmental disabilities/mental retardation agencies;
- A smaller percentage collaborate extensively with social services/welfare and vocational rehabilitation agencies, governors/state legislators, and voluntary organizations;
- Few states collaborate extensively with employers and insurers.

Program Participation

Core public health functions benefit the entire MCH population, namely all mothers and children, especially those with low incomes and/or limited access to health services. In 1991, there were approximately 4 million infants, 75.6 million children and adolescents, 45 million pregnant women and other women, and 3.9 million children with special health care needs.[55]

State data from 1991 show that among the 12.8 million women and children who received some direct care under Title V state programs, 755,000 were children with special health care needs.[56] These children represent about one-half of all children who are severely disabled and about 20 percent of those with chronic conditions. State CSHCN programs are the only public health programs with a dedicated focus to this population. There is wide variation by state, however, in the number of children served by CSHCN programs. This variation is the result of differences in agencies' historical service mission, the scope of covered services, federal and state funding patterns, overall state availability of health services, and participation in system development. These factors also explain why in many states, Title V CSHCN programs traditionally have not served children whose primary presenting condition is a behavioral, mental health, or psychiatric disorder.[57]

Expenditures

Fifteen percent of the first $600 million in annual appropriations are set aside by the Secretary of HHS for special projects of regional or national significance (SPRANS). In the past these funds have been used for many different purposes including screening for genetic disorders and sickle cell anemia, university-affiliated training programs for persons with developmental disabilities, national resource and technical centers, and parent support programs.

The remaining MCH funding is allocated to states based on a formula that takes into account the relative number of low-income children and the amounts of federal aid states received under several former categorical child health programs. To be eligible for MCH block grant funds, states must: (a) conduct a statewide needs assessment (done once every five years), (b) prepare a plan to meet the needs identified, and (c) provide a description of how MCH funds will be used. Since FY 1991, states have been required to devote at least 30 percent of their MCH funds to provide preventative and primary care services to children and at least 30 percent to children with special health care needs (in fact, just over 30 percent of state Title V expenditures go to children with special needs).[58] No more than 10 percent of funds can be used to cover administrative expenses.

In program year 1991, just over $499 million was allocated by the federal government to 59 state and local jurisdiction MCH programs. The Maternal and Child Health Bureau estimates that in 1991, 30 percent of the federal allocation went toward infrastructure building,

45 percent toward enabling services, and 25 percent toward basic medical and related health care services, including those for children with special health needs. As required, all states matched every four dollars in federal funds with three state dollars. Many states devoted three to four times the level of federal allocations to their MCH programs. State level Title V expenditures totaled $714 million in 1991.

MENTAL RETARDATION/DEVELOPMENTAL DISABILITY PROGRAMS[59]

Several federal and state programs provide services specifically to persons with mental retardation/developmental disabilities. These programs are:[60]

- Administration on Developmental Disabilities (ADD) programs. ADD is an agency in the Administration on Children and Families (ACF) in the U.S. Department of Health and Human Services.
- State and local mental retardation/developmental disabilities (MR/DD) programs.

State MR/DD programs are not directly tied to any federal agency. They receive federal funding through Medicaid or other programs, but do not receive any formula grant funds. Most of this discussion focuses on state programs, as they provide the majority of direct services.

Eligibility

MR/DD programs identify their target populations as persons with developmental disabilities. Although state programs are not operated specifically for children, children are included in their target population.

The term "developmental disabilities" requires some elaboration. Originally, at both the federal and state levels, programs were established specifically for persons with mental retardation. However, the scope of these programs was enlarged to include persons with related conditions, such as cerebral palsy and epilepsy, because these conditions also tended to have their onset in childhood and many persons with these conditions were also mentally retarded. Over time, the definition of persons to be assisted by these programs was further broadened to encompass all persons who had a disability that originated before age 22, and which caused significant functional difficulties in four or more of the following six areas of major life activity: self-care, understanding and use of language, learning, mobility, self-direction, or a capacity for independent living. The term "developmental disabilities" includes a wide range of physical and mental disabilities, including spinal cord injuries, heart conditions, and other conditions if they result in severe functional limitations.

As a result, state MR/DD agencies can, and to some extent do, serve individuals with conditions other than mental retardation. The focus of state MR/DD programs, however, remains on persons with mental retardation. These agencies are sometimes designated as MR/DD agencies. In some states, they may be designated only as developmental disabilities (DD) agencies.

Generally, any individual with developmental disabilities is eligible for services from MR/DD agencies regardless of age. However, a few states limit eligibility to adults. Moreover, in most states, children with developmental disabilities of school age will receive most services from the school system, so that persons served through MR/DD agencies are for the most part adults.

Administration

The Administration on Developmental Disabilities is not administratively linked to state MR/DD agencies nor do any federal ADD funds finance MR/DD agencies except indirectly through grants. Most of the federal funding used by MR/DD agencies comes through the Medicaid program, although federal funding sources also include the Social Services Block Grants.

Most service provision occurs through state MR/DD agencies. In most states, there are regional or county/city MR/DD agencies which manage the day-to-day operations of the agency. In some cases, the local government will provide additional funding to these agencies. In 1992, significant local and county funds were reported in at least 12 states.

Benefits/Services

ADMINISTRATION ON DEVELOPMENTAL DISABILITIES

The Federal Administration on Developmental Disabilities is composed of four programs:

- The Protection and Advocacy Program for People with Developmental Disabilities (PADD) which may directly advocate for all persons with developmental disabilities.
- The Basic State Grant Program which provides funds under a formula grant to Developmental Disabilities Councils in each state. These councils are designated by the governor and are independent of the MR/DD program. They are composed of the heads of relevant state agencies such as the Vocational Rehabilitation (VR) and MR/DD agencies as well as persons with developmental disabilities or their representatives. The DD Councils make grants to demonstrate new methods of providing services, conduct research, fill gaps in services, and in other ways improve the service system. The grants are typically time limited.
- The University Affiliated Program which awards funds to university based programs to conduct research, provide training, and provide services to persons with developmental disabilities.
- The Projects of National Significance Program which makes awards to colleges and universities and non-profit organizations for the purposes of conducting research and demonstrating improved methods of providing services to persons with developmental disabilities.

STATE MR/DD AGENCIES

The responsibilities of state MR/DD agencies vary from state to state. Traditionally, MR/DD agencies have primarily provided residential services. This includes large state-operated institutions (developmental centers, training centers, state schools, and designated MR/DD units in state psychiatric hospitals),[61] large privately operated residential facilities (intermediate care facilities and nursing homes), and smaller public and private residential facilities (intermediate care facilities and group homes).

Additional services are provided in the community and have become a larger part of MR/DD agency spending. These services include day habilitation or adult day care, aging services, assistive technology, early intervention, personal assistance, supported employment, and supported living services. Family support services, including case management, family counseling, respite care, home modification, equipment, in-home training, education, cash assistance, and other activities which improve the quality of life of persons with developmental disabilities are also provided by some MR/DD agencies.

Program Participation

The majority of information on who is served by MR/DD agencies is not separated by age. An extensive national survey of public spending for MR/DD[62] asks state MR/DD agencies (and other agencies where applicable) to gather data on participation and expenditures. Although not separated by age group, these data for 1992 are the most detailed and up-to-date information available. Here we report some of the overall numbers for adults and children, discuss a few important trends for adults and children together, and describe some attempts at developing separate estimates for children.

In 1992, 346,874 individuals received MR/DD services within residential settings. Slightly less than half (48 percent) were served in large residential settings (state or privately operated), defined as having 16 or more beds. The trend over time has been for many fewer individuals to be served in large out-of-home facilities and more individuals to be served in smaller community-based settings. In 1977, 71 percent of individuals receiving MR/DD residential services were in large (16 or more beds) settings while in 1992 this share dropped to 36 percent. A comparable increase has occurred in the smallest facilities (1 to 6 beds), from 7 percent in 1977 to 34 percent in 1992. This trend is also reflected in the decreasing number of residents in large state-operated institutions (and closures of these facilities) as well as in the increasing use of Medicaid ICF/MR funds for smaller residential settings.[63]

As with residential services, the provision of non-residential community-based services to persons with mental retardation and developmental disabilities has increased. A large part of this increase is the increased use of Home and Community-Based Services (HCBS) waivers in Medicaid to fund services.[64] In 1992, 63,206 individuals were served through HCBS waivers for persons with MR/DD. Family support programs administered by state MR/DD agencies also provide nonresidential services to families and are sometimes funded by HCBS waivers. In 1992, 47 states and the District of Columbia reported some family support initiative by MR/DD agencies. Seventeen states provided cash subsidy payments to a total of 12,300 families. Thirty-seven states provided respite care to 57,700 families, and the same number provided other general support to over 106,000 families.[65]

Information specifically on children is not available from most sources. However, Medicaid program information shows that 12,526 children under 21 received intermediate care facility services for mental retardation in 1993. This understates children receiving residential services since not all residential care facilities are captured in these numbers.[66] However, a rough approximation of children served is the number of children receiving ICF/MR services as a percent of all individuals receiving ICF/MR services—8 percent. It is even more difficult to estimate the number of children receiving community non-residential services: although some states limit services to adults, many provide services based on family need not age.

Expenditures

As with participation, most information on expenditures by MR/DD agencies is not reported by age. As before we first report total expenditures by state MR/DD agencies on all persons and from all funding sources, and then briefly present a rough approximation of MR/DD spending for children.

In addition to state MR/DD spending, federal spending by the ADD for FY 1994 was $115 million. Spending on the four main ADD programs discussed earlier is as follows: $69.3 million for state grants, $23.8 million for protection and advocacy, $3.7 million for special projects, and $18.3 million for university affiliated projects. This spending cannot be broken out by age group. Other federal funding for MR/DD programs, in particular Medicaid, is discussed as a source of funds for state programs.

State MR/DD program expenditures by source of funds for 1977 and 1992 are shown in Table 4.19. Expenditures are separated into two groups: spending for community services and large residential services (congregate 16 + beds). The latter is further separated into institutional services and large private residential services. Funding from federal and state sources is also reported.

Over time state MR/DD spending has increased from about $3.5 billion in 1977 to over $17 billion in 1992. Spending has been increasing as a proportion of total income as well, from $2.3 per $1,000 of personal income in 1977 to $3.3 in 1992. At the same time total spending has increased, spending on large residential services has fallen and spending on community-based services has risen. In 1977, three-quarters of MR/DD spending was for large residential services (over 16 beds). But by 1992, only 43 percent of total spending was for these services. As with participation, this reflects the trend toward smaller community-based residential settings. One of the major sources of funding for residential services is Medicaid payments for ICF/MR facilities. In 1977, only 2 percent of federal ICF/MR funds

Table 4.19 SOURCES OF TOTAL EXPENDITURES BY STATE MR/DD PROGRAMS
ON ADULTS AND CHILDREN BY SERVICE TYPE, 1977 AND 1992

	1977	1992
TOTAL FUNDS	$3,457,223,891	$17,277,897,592
CONGREGATE 16+ BEDS	2,585,224,129	7,388,126,858
INSTITUTIONAL SERVICES FUNDS	2,461,323,585	6,015,910,508
STATE FUNDS	1,821,619,787	2,999,472,783
General Funds	1,672,938,772	2,350,173,015
Local	8,440,740	5,971,973
Other State Funds	140,240,275	643,327,795
FEDERAL FUNDS	639,703,798	3,016,437,725
Federal ICF/MR	573,486,028	2,907,752,444
Title XX/SSBG Funds	4,865,000	483,412
Other Federal Funds	61,352,770	108,201,869
LARGE PRIVATE RESIDENTIAL	123,900,544	1,372,216,350
STATE FUNDS	90,726,880	677,920,574
General Funds	74,635,701	428,248,835
Other State Funds	12,650,179	235,652,278
Local/County Overmatch	3,441,000	14,019,461
FEDERAL FUNDS	33,173,664	694,295,776
Large Private ICF/MR	33,173,664	694,295,776
COMMUNITY SERVICES FUNDS	871,999,762	9,839,770,735
STATE FUNDS	675,812,391	6,590,360,915
General Funds	406,112,423	4,793,884,880
Other State Funds	60,221,787	922,241,863
Local/County Overmatch	63,687,253	508,922,595
SSI State Supplement	145,790,928	365,311,577
FEDERAL FUNDS	196,187,371	3,249,409,819
ICF/MR Funds	8,878,210	1,287,439,988
Small Public	0	241,817,846
Small Private	8,878,210	1,045,622,142
HCBS Waiver	0	876,812,080
Model 50/200 Waiver	0	12,177,903
Other Title XIX Programs	3,953,880	470,158,581
Title XX/SSBG Funds	154,869,273	202,002,180
Other Federal Funds	28,486,008	87,811,831
Waiver Clients' SSI/ADC	0	313,007,256

Source: Institute on Disability and Human Development (UAP), University of Illinois
at Chicago, 1994.

were spent on smaller residential settings compared to 26 percent in 1992. As the number of individuals served in institutions has decreased, total costs have not fallen proportionately because the daily costs per resident have increased. Daily costs per resident have increased (in 1992 dollars) from $45 in 1977 to $212 in 1992.

Over time federal Social Services Block Grant (SSBG Title XX) funds have become less important in funding MR/DD services, while HCBS waivers have become more important. Medicaid HCBS regular and model waivers fund approximately 5 percent of all state and local MR/DD spending.

The states have always played a larger role in funding MR/DD services than the federal government. In 1977, 25 percent of funds were from federal sources and in 1992, 40 percent were from federal sources. Federal sources are primarily Medicaid (96 percent in 1992), with a small amount of funding from SSBG and other funds. State funds are also primarily Medicaid matching funds. In 1992, of the more than $10 billion spent on MR/DD services, approximately 65 percent was covered through state-level Medicaid funds.[67] It follows that the majority of non-Medicaid funds is from state and local governments.

Expenditures on community services include small residential facilities and other community-based services. Expenditures on some of the important community service initiatives for children include $176 million on early intervention services, $7 million on assistive technology, and $279 million on family support initiatives.

All of these expenditures are for all persons served, both adults and children. It is difficult to separate spending by age, since most agencies do not separately report information or program services in this way. One way to estimate the percentage of total expenditures for children is to use the number of children receiving Medicaid payments for ICF/MR services as a percentage of all persons receiving these services. As reported above, this is 8 percent. This leads to an estimate of $557 million in federal spending for state MR/DD programs and $821 million in state spending. These are rough estimates, particularly for community-based services, and should be used only as a guideline for understanding the relative spending levels for children across programs.

MENTAL HEALTH PROGRAMS[68]

Both federal and state programs in a variety of agencies provide services to children with mental illness. These include general health service systems, special education services, and child welfare programs. In this section, we focus on programs designed specifically to provide mental health services. At the federal and state levels these programs are administered by:

- The Center for Mental Health Services (CMHS) which is an agency in the Substance Abuse and Mental Health Services Administration in the U.S. Department of Health and Human Services.
- State mental health agencies (SMHA). Programs and services provided by SMHAs are not directly tied to any federal agency. They receive federal funding through Medicaid or other federal sources, but do not receive any other formula grant funds.

Eligibility

The target population for mental health programs includes individuals with a variety of conditions including substance abuse, serious emotional disturbances, and a variety of disabilities or levels of functioning stemming from these conditions. Researchers have noted the varying definitions of serious emotional or behavioral disturbances among children used by different agencies serving children. Federal definitions put forward by the CMHS, Department of Education under IDEA, and the Head Start program differ from each other leading to different groups of children being eligible. For the most part, eligibility is related to the child's need, which is determined through diagnosis and having a level of impairment that limits functioning at home, school, or in the community.[69]

Programs administered by state mental health agencies may provide services to persons with developmental disabilities as well as mental illness, particularly in mental health hospitals. Usually these individuals are defined as dually diagnosed. Compared to MR/DD agencies, state mental health agencies tend to be more oriented toward treatment and amelioration of symptoms since mental illness is usually seen as a condition subject to improvement.

Administration

The federal government's role in mental health programs for children is through programs administered by the CMHS and through federal funding used by SMHAs. The majority of service provision occurs through state agencies. Federal funding for state agencies comes through Medicaid, Medicare, and the Alcohol, Drug Abuse, and Mental Health Services Block Grant.

The Alcohol, Drug Abuse, and Mental Health Administration Reorganization Act of 1992 mandated the creation of the national Center for Mental Health Services within the Substance Abuse and Mental Health Services Administration. Many of these services were previously housed in the National Institute of Mental Health (NIMH). NIMH is now an institute within the National Institutes of Health focusing on intramural and extramural research into issues related to mental health.

Benefits/Services

CENTER FOR MENTAL HEALTH SERVICES (CMHS)

This Center funds a number of activities for persons with mental illness. Since 1984, the Child and Adolescent Service System Program (CASSP) has offered grants to states for the purposes of improving interagency cooperation and coordination, developing infrastructure necessary for system improvement, and expanding the array of community-based services.

Currently, the Child Mental Health Services Initiative is offering state grants for Comprehensive Community Mental Health Services for Children with Serious Emotional Disturbance programs. The services provided under this initiative are community-based, noninstitutional, and family centered, emphasizing an interagency system of care approach. Sites receiving funding through this program are limited and are intended to be demonstration programs. This initiative is funded at $60 million for FY 1994.

The Protection and Advocacy Program for Mentally Ill Individuals (PAMII) serves people with mental illness in public and private residential facilities in cases of abuse, neglect, or violations of rights.

STATE MENTAL HEALTH AGENCIES

Mental health and substance abuse services include inpatient, residential, outpatient, and emergency services. State mental health agencies often run state psychiatric hospitals. They also provide funding for residential treatment centers for emotionally disturbed children, and county psychiatric hospitals. Outpatient services include day treatment, case management, and mobile crisis teams. These services are provided in part by ambulatory mental health organizations, including those formerly classified as community mental health centers. Exact services vary substantially among mental health agencies across states.

Program Participation

Data on the number of children receiving mental health services are not regularly collected. Studies indicate that anywhere from 6 to 33 percent of children with a diagnosable mental disorder receive some type of mental health service in the previous year. And these services are most often provided through the schools. Fewer young people receive services in a mental health setting that would fall under the aegis of SMHAs.[70]

A study conducted by the CMHS provides information on the number of children under 18 on the rolls of mental health organizations at the end of 1988. These numbers are shown in Table 4.20. Over 25,000 children and adolescents received inpatient or residential mental health services at the end of 1988. The majority of children and adolescents are being served by private psychiatric hospitals which

Table 4.20 NUMBER AND PERCENT OF CHILDREN UNDER 18 ON ROLLS OF MENTAL HEALTH ORGANIZATIONS, BY TYPE OF PROGRAM AND ORGANIZATION (END OF YEAR, 1988)

| Program Element | Type of Organization | | |
	State and County Mental Hospitals	Private Psychiatric Hospitals	Non-Federal General Hospitals
Inpatient Services			
Total on rolls	100,815	28,046	35,609
Under 18	7,449	11,612	5,962
Percent under 18	7%	41%	17%
Residential Treatment			
Total on rolls	812	1,662	NA
Under 18	168	1,263	NA
Percent under 18	20%	76%	NA
Outpatient Services			
Total on rolls	97,149	109,275	323,339
Under 18	12,229	28,350	76,653
Percent under 18	13%	26%	24%
Partial Care			
Total on rolls	17,478	7,986	15,726
Under 18	1,607	2,200	2,391
Percent under 18	9%	28%	15%

Source: Reproduced from Kimberly Hoagwood and Agnes Rupp, "Mental Health Service Needs, Use, and Costs for Children and Adolescents with Mental Disorders and their Families: Preliminary Evidence," Table 4.2 in Center for Mental Health Services, *Mental Health United States, 1994*, R.W. Manderscheid and M.A. Sonnenchien (eds.), DHHS Pub. No. (SMA) 94-3000, Washington, D.C., 1994. Original source is published and unpublished inventory data from the Statistical Analysis Branch, Division of State and Community Systems Development, Center for Mental Health Services.

receive most of their funding from private insurance. Over 120,000 children and adolescents were receiving outpatient services or partial care services at the end of 1988. These numbers are an underestimate of the number of children served over the entire year.

As with MR/DD services, there has been a decrease over time in the number of persons (of any age) served in state-operated mental health institutions, from about 500,000 persons in 1960 to about 150,000 persons in 1988. Unlike trends in MR/DD services, there has only been "limited development of supported community living" for persons with mental illness.[71]

Expenditures

The expenditures made by SMHAs are not easily separable by age. We first discuss total SMHA spending on all services, and then discuss available information on spending for children and adolescents.[72] The most recent data on expenditures are from 1990.

Total expenditures by SMHAs in 1990 were $12 billion. In constant dollars, spending remained flat from 1981 to 1990, increasing by less than 2 percent over that period. Spending varied across states. Per capita spending in 1990 ranged from over $100 in Delaware and New York to around $20 in Indiana, Idaho, and Utah. Expenditures can be separated into three categories: state psychiatric and other hospitals, community-based programs, and other functions including prevention, research, training, and administration. The majority of state funds in 1990 (58 percent) were spent on state-operated psychiatric hospitals, with only 1 percent of total funds going to other hospitals. Spending for state-operated hospitals also varied across states, from 85 percent of Iowa's spending to 27 percent of spending in Wisconsin. Community-based programs received 38 percent of total funds. For those states who report expenditures by service setting, inpatient care expenditures have fallen by 8 percent in constant dollars since 1981, while spending on residential care services has increased by 156 percent and on ambulatory care services has increased by 81 percent.

Growth in spending on community-based services has been relatively slow compared to growth in community-based MR/DD services. In part this is because there is less access to federal revenues for these services. Mentally ill persons cannot receive Medicaid payments through the ICF/MR program. Medicaid does not cover the cost of psychiatric hospitals for individuals between the ages of 22 and 64. Also, there are currently no Medicaid Home and Community-Based

Services waivers targeted toward mentally ill children, as there are for children with mental retardation and developmental disabilities.[73]

The source of most funding for SMHAs is from state governments. In 1990, this source accounted for 80 percent of all SMHA mental health revenues. Federal government sources accounted for 15 percent of total revenues, including 9 percent from Medicaid, 2.4 percent from the Alcohol, Drug Abuse, and Mental Health Services Block Grant, and 3 percent from Medicare. Other funds include 2 percent from local governments.

The difficulty in gathering information on expenditures for children is that not all states were able to allocate all spending by age. Some states were unable to allocate any spending separately by age. Table 4.21 reports, by state, SMHA 1990 expenditures for children and adolescents. It also includes the percent of total expenditures that were unallocated by age to give an idea of the extent of this problem. In general, allocating community expenditures by age was more difficult than allocating state mental health hospital expenditures.

In 1990, approximately 10 percent of total national SMHA spending, or $1.2 billion, was spent on services for children and adolescents. However, this is only a rough estimate nationally since 48 percent of total spending was unallocated by age. Spending per capita for children varied across states from less than $5 per capita in Montana, Ohio, and South Dakota to over $40 per capita in New York, Massachusetts, Michigan, and the District of Columbia.

HEAD START

Head Start, with the aid of direct participation of parents in the program, provides comprehensive developmental services for low-income preschool-aged children. The program is designed to strengthen the abilities of disadvantaged children to succeed in school and in later life. Since its inception in 1965, Head Start has provided educational, social, medical, dental, nutritional, and mental health services to almost 15 million children and their families.

Eligibility

The Head Start statute requires that at least 90 percent of children served by the program come from families with incomes at or below the federal poverty guidelines or from families receiving AFDC. Chil-

Table 4.21 EXPENDITURES BY STATE MENTAL HEALTH AGENCIES FOR
CHILDREN, BY STATE, 1990

State	Spending on Children and Adolescents	Spending on Children and Adolescents Per Capita	% of Total Spending on Children and Adolescents	% of Total Spending Unallocated by Age
Alabama	N/A	N/A	N/A	100%
Alaska	N/A	N/A	N/A	100%
Arizona	$17,984,054	$18.33	18%	47%
Arkansas	$6,279,759	$10.11	10%	2%
California	$203,666,925	$26.28	16%	13%
Colorado	$10,138,563	$11.77	9%	76%
Connecticut	*	*	*	*
Delaware	*	*	*	*
District of Columbia	$13,009,662	$111.11	8%	66%
Florida	$53,726,544	$18.74	11%	89%
Georgia	$15,164,866	$8.78	5%	71%
Hawaii	$8,324,448	$29.72	20%	80%
Idaho	$2,884,600	$9.35	14%	43%
Illinois	$57,452,500	$19.50	15%	6%
Indiana	$35,087,097	$24.10	13%	87%
Iowa	$8,493,640	$11.82	18%	15%
Kansas	$21,768,353	$32.90	25%	14%
Kentucky	N/A	N/A	N/A	100%
Louisiana	$22,561,839	$18.38	19%	4%
Maine	$10,483,604	$33.93	13%	3%
Maryland	$26,676,141	$24.67	10%	59%
Massachusetts	$57,742,756	$42.68	11%	89%
Michigan	$117,623,704	$47.92	17%	10%
Minnesota	$36,269,098	$31.08	15%	0%
Mississippi	N/A	N/A	N/A	100%
Missouri	$14,667,654	$11.16	8%	24%
Montana	$636,199	$2.86	3%	14%
Nebraska	$4,006,863	$9.34	9%	24%
Nevada	$8,079,075	$27.21	20%	12%
New Hampshire	$4,521,823	$16.22	8%	39%

(continued)

dren found to be eligible remain eligible throughout the program year
in which they are enrolled and the immediately succeeding program
year regardless of any changes in family income.

In addition to the income requirements, every Head Start program
is required to make at least 10 percent of its enrollment slots available
to children with disabilities. Only children who are disabled (as defined in the legislation) *and* who because of their disability require
special education and related services, are counted toward the

Table 4.21 EXPENDITURES BY STATE MENTAL HEALTH AGENCIES FOR
CHILDREN BY STATE, 1990 (continued)

State	Spending on Children and Adolescents	Spending on Children and Adolescents Per Capita	% of Total Spending on Children and Adolescents	% of Total Spending Unallocated by Age
New Jersey	$35,706,000	$19.84	8%	66%
New Mexico	N/A	N/A	N/A	100%
New York	$171,531,448	$40.27	8%	73%
North Carolina	$18,064,795	$11.25	6%	43%
North Dakota	$1,492,768	$6.51	6%	100%
Ohio	$11,680,671	$4.17	3%	97%
Oklahoma	$9,624,933	$11.50	9%	7%
Oregon	$11,198,239	$13.46	10%	5%
Pennsylvania	$28,825,000	$10.31	4%	36%
Rhode Island	*	*	*	*
South Carolina	$16,989,097	$18.46	10%	6%
South Dakota	$593,633	$2.99	4%	47%
Tennessee	$32,545,894	$26.75	23%	5%
Texas	$41,922,068	$8.67	11%	N/A
Utah	$4,020,727	$6.41	11%	50%
Vermont	$3,447,626	$24.10	11%	4%
Virginia	$16,697,950	$11.10	6%	29%
Washington	$23,547,031	$18.67	11%	21%
West Virginia	N/A	N/A	N/A	100%
Wisconsin	$11,324,538	$8.79	8%	74%
Wyoming	N/A	N/A	N/A	23%
Total	$1,200,004,188	$19.74	10%	48%

N/A = Services provided but exact expenditures unallocatable. * = responsibility for
child mental health services under a state agency other than Mental Health.
Source: Theodore Lutterman, Vera Hollen, and Michael Hogan, "Funding Sources and
Expenditures of State Mental Health Agencies: Revenue/Expenditure Study Results
Fiscal Year 1990," National Association of State Mental Health Program Directors Re-
search Institute, Alexandria, Va., March 1993.

10-percent Congressionally mandated enrollment opportunities requirement.[74]

Administration

Head Start is administered by the U.S. Department of Health and
Human Services. States have only a modest advisory role, although
local governments are sometimes selected to operate Head Start programs. At the community level, each program is run by a Head Start
grantee. Grants are awarded by Department of Health and Human
Services Regional Offices (and the Administration on Children and

Families' Native American and Migrant Program Branches) to local public agencies, private non-profit organizations, and school systems.

Benefits/Services

In addition to receiving the full range of Head Start development services (education, parent involvement, social services, and nutritional and health services), children with disabilities receive special education and related services. Among the special services provided to children with disabilities by Head Start staff are individualized teaching, speech therapy and language stimulation, and transportation. Services provided to Head Start children through collaborating agencies include medical and psychological diagnosis, evaluation or testing, and medical treatment.[75]

Each Head Start program is required to conduct a community needs assessment and to coordinate with other service providers in the community in order to save scarce resources. By statute, Head Start programs are required to establish procedures for obtaining payment from other services providers or agencies responsible for providing or paying for certain types of services. Over one-half of Head Start children, for example, receive medical and dental services paid for by Medicaid/EPSDT.

Program Participation

In FY 1993, Head Start served over 713,903 children. Although Head Start programs are required to make at least 10 percent of their enrollment slots available to children with disabilities, over 13 percent (or 94,000 children) of all children enrolled in Head Start in 1993 had a disability. The number of children with disabilities served increased from 69,267 in 1990 to 94,235 in 1993—an increase of almost 25,000 children.

The distribution of children with disabilities in Head Start, by primary disabling condition, is as follows: 69.5 percent speech impaired, 10.2 percent health impaired, 6.0 percent specific learning disability, 4.6 percent seriously emotionally disturbed, 3.5 percent physically disabled, 3.1 percent mentally retarded, 1.6 percent hearing impaired, 1.4 percent visually impaired, 0.1 percent blind, and 0.1 percent deaf. Just over 14 percent of children with disabilities enrolled in Head Start programs had multiple disabling conditions. This is a slight decrease from the corresponding figure for 1990, 15.5 percent.

Expenditures

Approximately $2.78 billion was spent by the federal government in FY 1993 to operate Head Start programs. Grantees are required to provide matching funds for 20 percent of the total costs of the program. This matching share may be in cash or in-kind, and the requirement may be waived wholly or in part under certain conditions. There are no minimum or maximum requirements on the level of funds that Head Start grantees can devote to supplemental services for children with disabilities. Drawing on detailed grantee applications, the Head Start Bureau estimates that approximately 3.3 percent of total Head Start expenditures are for additional services for children with disabilities (that is, for services provided to supplement those received by all Head Start children).

FAMILY SUPPORT PROGRAMS

Historically, families were encouraged by medical and social service professionals to place children born with severe disabilities in institutional settings. More recently, recognition of the importance of family, along with advocacy efforts for financial support of necessary services, has led to greater numbers of children with severe disabilities living with their families. The family support movement has also led to further efforts to initiate or expand the support and services available to families caring for children with mental retardation or other disabilities.

Today, a number of states have developed formal family support programs. The major goals of these programs are "to deter unnecessary out-of-home placements, return persons living in institutions back to families, and enhance the care giving capacity of families."[76] These programs vary across states in services provided, level and type of funding, who is served, and in what agency the program is located.

This section gives a general overview of these programs. While the programs described here are to some extent a subset of programs offered by MR/DD agencies, they are described separately to highlight their specific purpose.

Eligibility

Most states have relatively broad eligibility criteria for their family support programs. The basic criteria are based on a diagnosis of de-

velopmental disabilities, although some states have a narrower definition restricted to a few conditions. Programs usually attach some
additional criteria for severity of disability to limit eligibility. While
many state family support programs are targeted to children, only 12
states in 1989 limited services to this group.

Administration

Administration of family support programs varies across states. Some
states have dedicated funding through the state agency that provides
services for persons with developmental disabilities, while others are
experimenting with pilot or demonstration projects funded by Developmental Disability Councils or other groups.

Benefits/Services

There are many different services provided by family support programs. These fall into three different groups: services, case manage-
ment/service coordination, and financial assistance.[77] Table 4.22
shows which state programs offered financial assistance or services.
We also list states that have limited programs that cover only respite
services.

Services are further grouped into core services and traditional developmental services. Core services include respite and child care,
recreation, support services/counseling, training, in-home assistance
(such as home health care or attendant care), environmental adapta-
tions (such as adaptive equipment or home/vehicle modifications),
information/referral and advocacy services, and other special needs
(such as transportation, special diet or clothing, health insurance,
rent assistance, home repairs, and utilities). Traditional developmental services include medical services, nursing services, speech,
occupational, or physical therapy, and behavior management. Many
children receive these services through their schools.

In 1989, twenty-five state family support programs provided financial assistance of some kind. Financial assistance programs provide
either cash subsidies or some payment for specific services in the form
of allowances, vouchers, reimbursement of certain spending, lines of
credit. Even with provision of cash subsidies, states may require re-
ceipts to document use of subsidies for allowed expenditures.

Table 4.22 STATE FAMILY SUPPORT EFFORT PER $1,000 OF PERSONAL
INCOME, 1989

Rank	State	Total Family Support Effort ($)	Family Support per $1,000 of Personal Income ($)
1	North Dakota	3,977,000	0.4419
2	Montana	2,547,203	0.2547
3	New Hampshire	3,712,270	0.1856
4	Massachusetts	18,500,000	0.1581
5	Rhode Island	1,867,000	0.1167
6	Michigan	14,679,251	0.0985
7	Maine	1,500,000	0.0882
8	Alaska	718,000	0.0718
9	New York	22,500,000	0.0688
10	Vermont	544,150	0.0680
11	Pennsylvania	12,000,000	0.0638
12	California	30,511,839	0.0597
13	Florida	11,285,234	0.0579
14	New Jersey[a]	8,793,000	0.0539
15	Missouri[a]	3,638,053	0.0472
16	Arizona	2,349,600	0.0470
17	Maryland	4,000,000	0.0465
18	Louisiana[b]	1,804,378	0.0347
19	Washington	2,500,000	0.0338
20	Ohio	4,777,305	0.0295
21	Wisconsin	1,971,000	0.0270
22	Kentucky[a]	1,211,814	0.0258
23	Illinois	4,720,000	0.0240
24	Utah	447,100	0.0224
25	Connecticut	1,373,472	0.0193
26	Texas	4,315,000	0.0179
27	Minnesota	1,128,700	0.0161

(continued)

Program Participation

Only a limited number of families actually receive services under
these programs. In 1989 approximately 130,000 families received
some family support services. The largest family support efforts are
in California (25,000 families served), New York (24,000), Pennsyl-
vania (15,000), Florida (11,000), and Massachusetts (10,000).

Expenditures

Nationally, family support efforts represent about 2 percent of total
1990 budgets for persons with developmental disabilities.[78] Table 4.23
lists state family support spending by state, and spending per $1,000

Table 4.22 STATE FAMILY SUPPORT EFFORT PER $1,000 OF PERSONAL
INCOME, 1989 (*continued*)

Rank	State	Total Family Support Effort ($)	Family Support per $1,000 of Personal Income ($)
28	Nevada	244,478	0.0144
29	Arkansas	400,000	0.0143
30	Nebraska	300,000	0.0125
31	New Mexico	187,000	0.0104
32	Idaho	120,000	0.0100
33	Iowa	400,000	0.0098
34	North Carolina[a]	812,311	0.0091
35	Oregon[b]	305,000	0.0076
36	Delaware	75,000	0.0068
37	Georgia	611,562	0.0066
38	Colorado	343,000	0.0065
39	Hawaii	115,000	0.0064
40	Alabama[b]	325,000	0.0064
41	Wyoming	37,800	0.0063
42	Indiana	434,535	0.0054
43	South Carolina	220,000	0.0051
44	Virginia	175,000	0.0017
45	Tennessee	108,000	0.0017

Note: Kansas, Mississippi, Oklahoma, South Dakota, and West Virginia did not have any spending on family support programs.
a. While not a family support initiative, a portion of these funds provides services to families.
b. A portion of this state's family support effort is financed with Developmental Disabilities Council funds.
Source: Valerie Bradley, James Knoll, and John Agosta, *Emerging Issues in Family Support*, AAMR Monographs, 1992, Table 3.4.

of personal income. This varies from $0.44 in North Dakota to $0.002 in Tennessee. Five states (Kansas, Mississippi, Oklahoma, South Dakota, and West Virginia) did not have any spending in 1989 on family support programs. These expenditures show the wide diversity in size of family support programs. Overall, family support programs are a small portion of spending on children with disabilities. However, these programs are important because they reveal that the needs of all children with disabilities are not being fully met by other programs.

Notes

1. For a list of federal laws and programs relevant to persons with disabilities see U.S. Department of Education, Office of Special Education and Rehabilitative Services,

Table 4.23 SELECTED FAMILY SUPPORT SERVICES AND PROGRAM TYPES,
          BY STATE, 1989

State	Financial Assistance	Services	Respite Only
Alabama	-	-	x
Alaska	-	x	-
Arizona	x	x	-
Arkansas	x	-	-
California	-	x	-
Colorado	x	-	-
Connecticut	x	x	-
Delaware	-	-	x
Florida	-	x	-
Georgia	-	x	-
Hawaii	x	-	-
Idaho	x	x	-
Illinois	x	x	-
Indiana	-	x	-
Iowa	x	-	-
Kansas	-	(a)	-
Kentucky	-	x	-
Louisiana	x	x	-
Maine	-	x	-
Maryland	-	x	-
Massachusetts	-	x	-
Michigan	x	x	-
Minnesota	x	x	-
Mississippi	-	(a)	-
Missouri	-	(a)	-
Montana	x	x	-
Nebraska	x	-	-
Nevada	x	x	-

(continued)

Summary of Existing Legislation Affecting People with Disabilities, Washington, D.C., June 1992.

2. National Academy of Social Insurance, *Preliminary Status Report of the Disability Policy Panel*, Washington, D.C., 1994, contains additional details on the legislative history of the SSI program.

3. This definition is largely the same as that used for the DI program.

4. See General Accounting Office, "Social Security: Rapid Rise in Children on SSI Disability Rolls Follows New Regulations," September 1994, Report No. HEHS-94-225 for discussion of the relative importance of these two effects on child SSI caseloads. Concern about whether these programmatic changes have led to increased "coaching" of children to qualify for SSI benefits is addressed in Social Security Administration, "Findings from the Study of Title XVI Childhood Disability Claims," May 1994. The study finds "no evidence of widespread coaching or malingering."

5. Family income excludes income counted in AFDC eligibility. Some states' SSI programs provide higher benefits to individuals whose federal SSI benefits are cut under this provision.

Table 4.23 SELECTED FAMILY SUPPORT SERVICES AND PROGRAM TYPES,
BY STATE, 1989 (*continued*)

State	Financial Assistance	Services	Respite Only
New Hampshire	x	x	-
New Jersey	-	(a)	-
New Mexico	-	-	x
New York	-	x	-
North Carolina	-	(a)	-
North Dakota	x	x	-
Ohio	x	-	-
Oklahoma	-	-	-
Oregon	x	x	-
Pennsylvania	x	x	-
Rhode Island	x	x	-
South Carolina	x	x	-
South Dakota	-	-	-
Tennessee	-	x	-
Texas	x	-	-
Utah	-	x	-
Vermont	-	-	x
Virginia	x	x	-
Washington	-	x	-
West Virginia	-	(a)	-
Wisconsin	x	x	-
Wyoming	x	-	-

(a) Although these states did not identify family support as a specific priority, some services were available to families.
Source: Valerie Bradley, James Knoll, and John Agosta, *Emerging Issues in Family Support*, AAMR Monographs, 1992, Table 3.2.

6. Although states may choose to provide any level of optional supplementation, states are required to provide at least supplemental payments to maintain income levels of recipients transferred to the SSI program from a state program at the inception of SSI in 1974.

7. Office of Supplemental Security Income Policy, Social Security Administration "Children Receiving SSI," Washington, D.C., December 1994.

8. U.S. Department of Health and Human Services, Office of Inspector General, "Concerns about the Participation of Children with Disabilities in the Supplemental Security Income Program," Washington, D.C., October 1994.

9. This section draws on discussion in Association of Maternal and Child Health Programs, "MCH Related Federal Programs: Legal Handbook for Program Planners, Supplemental Security Income (SSI) for Disabled Children," Washington, D.C., August 1991.

10. These numbers are from a 10-percent sample of SSI administrative data. Large survey samples, including the Survey of Income and Program Participation (SIPP), Current Population Survey (CPS), and National Health Interview Survey (NHIS), also report participation in SSI although some of this information is limited. For example,

the SIPP asks families if they receive any income from SSI and asks adults whether they participate in SSI, but does not ask the participation question separately for each child. Therefore, we cannot measure child participation in SSI from SIPP.

11. In a new program, caseload growth can occur even if the number of new awards each year is constant because rates of leaving the program are lower than new awards. However, new SSI awards to children have increased in recent years.

12. As part of the *Zebley* decision, SSA reconsidered all child eligibility determinations made from January 1980 through February 1991. Therefore, some of this increase is readjudication of cases that had previously been denied and some are new applications. Of the 287,900 children who had their cases reevaluated through March 1994, 45 percent have been found eligible. See General Accounting Office, "Social Security: Rapid Rise in Children on SSI Disability Rolls Follows New Regulations," Washington, D.C., September 1994, Report No. HEHS-94-225.

13. Information for the discussion of characteristics and diagnoses comes from the Office of Supplemental Security Income, Social Security Administration, "Children Receiving SSI," Washington, D.C., December 1994.

14. These figures reflect the diagnosis by which the child was deemed eligible for SSI (this may or may not be the primary medical diagnosis). Many children have multiple diagnoses, but the table reflects only one diagnosis per child. The statistics do not reflect the number of all children in the population with a certain diagnostic condition because not all children are eligible for SSI.

15. Kalman Rupp and Charles Scott, "Length of Stay on the Supplemental Security Income (SSI) Disability Program," *Social Security Bulletin*, Spring 1995.

16. Since annual SSI payments for blind and disabled children over time are not available, annual payments shown in Table 4.5 are calculated as December payments multiplied by 12. This estimate is fairly accurate as shown by comparing our estimate for 1993 of total federally administered payments (federal SSI payments plus federally administered state supplementation payments), $4.26 billion, to the actual number, $4.35 billion, reported to us in conversations with individuals at SSA. We estimate state administered supplementation for blind and disabled children by assuming the same ratio of state administered to total state supplementation for children as for all blind and disabled individuals.

17. If, at 1993 caseload levels, real per capita payments had remained at 1989 levels, total expenditures on blind and disabled children would have been $3.9 billion, $400 million less than actual expenditures.

18. Because the caseload of children on SSI changes from month to month, total payments per child on SSI reported here are only estimates. They are calculated as total annual real payments (from Table 4.5) divided by total blind and disabled child caseload for December of the respective year.

19. Information for the discussion in this section is drawn from Congressional Research Service, *Medicaid Source Book: Background Data and Analysis*, Washington, D.C., January 1993.

20. House Committee on Ways and Means, *Overview of Entitlement Programs*, Washington, D.C., July 1994.

21. In addition to medically needy programs, states have the option of using the so-called 300-percent rule for eligibility for those requiring institutional care whose income is above the SSI eligibility level. This program allows eligibility for those who require institutional care, meet the state resource requirements, and whose income does not exceed three times the basic SSI payment level. Income applied to this standard must be gross income with no deductions allowed. States may use a lower cut-off level. In 1991, 35 states used the 300-percent rule option. Of these states, 17 did not have a

medically needy program for those requiring institutional care. Two states, Missouri and Illinois, have neither a medically needy program nor do they use the 300-percent rule for those needing institutional care. In these states individuals may qualify for Medicaid under the spend down provisions required of states that do not automatically provide Medicaid to SSI recipients.

22. Sally Bachman and Brian Burwell, "Medicaid Home and Community Based Services for Children with Disabilities," technical memorandum for the U.S. Department of Health and Human Services, Washington, D.C., October 1994.

23. States that have medically needy programs may offer a more restrictive set of services to this group.

24. Data on individual Medicaid payments can be used to examine participation and expenditures for all children with disabilities defined by service use, expenditure level, or diagnostic group. One study by Marilyn Ellwood and Elicia Herz, "Longitudinal Analysis of High Cost Medicaid Children in California," Systemetrics, October 1990, finds for California that of all children on Medicaid with expenditures of $25,000 or more in 1983, more than 25 percent were eligible through some criterion other than SSI or institutionalization. These results are not nationally representative, but suggest that the numbers reported in this background report may indeed underestimate participation and expenditures. On-going studies are attempting to examine expenditures for children eligible through SSI versus expenditures for all children with high costs.

25. Data for Arizona and Rhode Island are not included. Arizona's program is run under a waiver and Rhode Island did not report the information used.

26. These expenditures may understate total Medicaid expenditures on children with disabilities for the same reasons reported participation numbers may be understated.

27. Marilyn Rymer Ellwood, "SSI-Related Disabled Children and Medicaid," prepared for the U.S. Department of Health and Human Services, Office of Family, Community and Long-term Care Policy, Washington, D.C., June 1990.

28. Information for TEFRA and HCBS waivers from Sally Bachman and Brian Burwell, "Medicaid Home and Community Based Services for Children with Disabilities," technical memorandum for the U.S. Department of Health and Human Services, Washington, D.C., October 1994.

29. Prior to 1990, this Act was known as the "Education of the Handicapped Act."

30. Note that the Chapter 1 (SOP) program enabled states to receive funds for children with disabilities from birth through age 21, while Part B authorizes state grants based on the number of children with disabilities aged 3 to 21.

31. National Association of School Psychologists, "Assessment and Eligibility in Special Education: An Examination of Policy and Practice with Proposals for Change," Project FORUM, National Association of State Directors of Special Education, Alexandria, Va., July 1994.

32. Richard Allington, "Unintended Effects of Educational Reform in New York," *Educational Policy*, Vol. 6, No. 4, pp. 397–414, December 1992.

33. The difficulties associated with current assessment procedures in special education are drawn from Margaret J. McLaughlin, Patricia F. Schofield, and Sandra H. Warren, "Educational Reform: Issues for the Inclusion of Students with Disabilities," in M. Couthinho and A. Repp (eds.), *Enhancing the Integration of Children with Disabilities*, forthcoming, Baltimore: Brookes/Cole.

34. The Office of Special Education and Rehabilitative Services does not collect disability information for children under age 6.

These 4.6 million special education students were served by 308,904 FTE special education teachers and 311,490 FTE staff other than teachers. These figures do not include regular classroom teachers (2,148,833) and other staff who provide services to students with and without disabilities as part of the general education program.

35. Although they are not well understood, the relationships between disability, race/ethnicity, and poverty are a topic of much current interest and study. See, for example, Patricia Kirkpatrick, "Triple Jeopardy: Disability, Race, and Poverty in America," *Poverty and Race*, Vol. 3, No. 3, Poverty and Race Research Action Council, May/June 1994.

36. In addition, $325.8 million was appropriated to states in FY 1993 to serve approximately 442,000 preschoolers with disabilities. The per-child allocation under the preschool grant ($738) along with the per-child award from Part B ($411) meant that each state was given approximately $1,149 under IDEA for each preschooler receiving special education and related services (counted as of December 1 of the preceding year).

37. Stephen Chaikind, Louis C. Danielson, and Marsha L. Brauen, "What Do We Know About the Costs of Special Education? A Selected Review," *The Journal of Special Education*, Vol. 26, No. 4, 1993, pp. 344–370.

38. Mary T. Moore, E. William Strang, Myron Schwartz, and Mark Braddock, *Patterns in Special Education Service Delivery and Cost* (U.S. Department of Education Contract No. 300-84-0257), Decision Resources Corporation, Washington, D.C., December 1988.

39. Trina Osher, John George, and Patricia Gonzalez, "A Resource Paper on the Relative Cost of Special Education," Project FORUM, National Association of State Directors of Special Education, Alexandria, Va., June 27, 1991.

40. U.S. Department of Education, Office of Special Education and Rehabilitative Services, *Summary of Existing Legislation Affecting People with Disabilities*, Washington, D.C., June 1992.

41. This description is drawn from "Building Systems: A Report on Title V Programs' Collaboration with the Part H Early Intervention Initiative," Association of Maternal and Child Health Programs, Washington, D.C., December 1993.

42. U.S. Department of Education, *To Assure the Free Appropriate Public Education of All Children with Disabilities, Sixteenth Annual Report to Congress on the Implementation of The Individuals with Disabilities Education Act*, Washington, D.C., 1994.

43. Several states are relying on substantial collections from private insurers to finance Part H services. Massachusetts, for example, requires that private insurance companies cover the costs of early intervention services.

44. Catherine Sonnier, *Implementing Early Intervention Services for Infants and Toddlers with Disabilities (P.L. 101-476, Part H)*, National Conference of State Legislatures, Denver, Colorado, May 1991.

45. Catherine Sonnier, *Implementing Early Intervention Services for Infants and Toddlers with Disabilities (P.L. 101-476, Part H)*, National Conference of State Legislatures, Denver, Colorado, May 1991.

46. Conversations with Tom Coakley, Technical Assistance Coordinator, National Early Childhood Technical Assistance System, Chapel Hill, North Carolina.

47. For a summary of these cost studies, see Deborah F. Perry, "Projecting the Costs of Early Intervention Services: Four States' Experiences," National Early Childhood Technical Assistance System, Chapel Hill, North Carolina, September 1993.

48. See Catherine Sonnier, Chapter Two: The Costs and Benefits of Early Intervention, in *Implementing Early Intervention Services for Infants and Toddlers with Disabilities (P.L. 101-476, Part H)*, National Conference of State Legislatures, Denver, Colorado, May 1991.

49. Much of this description is based on U.S. Department of Education, Office of Special Education and Rehabilitative Services, *Summary of Existing Legislation Affecting People with Disabilities*, Washington, D.C., June 1992.

50. For a state by state review of these criteria, see John G. Reiss, "State Title V CSHCN Programs: Eligibility Criteria and Scope of Services," Institute for Child Health Policy, Gainesville, Fl., January 1994.

51. These 10 states (Alabama, Arkansas, Florida, Illinois, Iowa, Kentucky, Nebraska, North Dakota, Oklahoma, and Oregon) were allowed to maintain their previously established structure when their programs, along with the six related categorical health programs for mothers and children, were consolidated.

52. Draft Survey Report, "Measuring State Title V Progress in Implementing the National Objective on Systems Development for Children with Chronic and Disabling Conditions," prepared by Margaret M. McManus, J. Dunbar, P. Newacheck, and H. Fox, July 1993.

53. These survey findings from the Maternal and Child Health Policy Research Center are summarized in "State Title V Programs' Progress in Developing Systems of Care for Children with Special Health Care Needs," Association of Maternal and Child Health Programs, Washington, D.C., undated.

54. Respite care is even provided by 19 states.

55. Maternal and Child Health Bureau, *Report to Congress on Fiscal Year 1991: Maternal and Child Health Activities and Health Status*, Health Resources and Services Administration, Public Health Service, U.S. Department of Health and Human Services, Rockville, Md., January 1995.

56. Results from the Maternal and Child Health Policy Research Center's Survey of state CSHCN programs reports a slightly lower number for 1991, 737,000 children or between 1 and 2 percent of the total child population.

57. Personal communication with Dr. John Reiss, Director, Institute for Child Health Policy. For states' listings of excluded medical conditions, including behavioral, mental health, and psychiatric disorders, see John G. Reiss, "State Title V CSHCN Programs: Eligibility Criteria and Scope of Services," Institute for Child Health Policy, Gainesville, Fl., January 1994.

58. Maternal and Child Health Bureau, *Report to Congress on Fiscal Year 1991: Maternal and Child Health Activities and Health Status*, Health Resources and Services Administration, Public Health Service, U.S. Department of Health and Human Services, Rockville, Md., January 1995.

59. We gratefully acknowledge Dr. Ronald Conley's contributions to this section.

60. Other state and federal programs, in particular special education programs, also provide services to children with MR/DD.

61. In some states institutions are administered by a separate organization.

62. David Braddock, Richard Hemp, Lynn Bachelder, and Glenn Fujiura, *The State of the States in Developmental Disabilities*, Institute on Disability and Human Development, The University of Illinois at Chicago, October 1994.

63. K.C. Lakin and M.J. Hall, "Medicaid-financed Residential Care for Persons with Mental Retardation," *Health Care Financing Review*, annual supplement, 1990.

64. HCBS waivers can be used for target populations other than individuals with mental retardation or developmental disabilities. The numbers discussed here are for MR/DD waivers only. See the Medicaid section for additional detail on the HCBS program.

65. David Braddock, Richard Hemp, Lynn Bachelder, and Glenn Fujiura, *The State of the States in Developmental Disabilities*, Institute on Disability and Human Development, The University of Illinois at Chicago, October 1994.
These numbers are approximate because of the differences in reporting systems

across states and because not all states provided information in all categories. Category counts may reflect duplication of families in more than one category and are for services to all age groups.

66. Of all adults and children receiving MR/DD services in residential settings of any size, roughly half were in non-ICF/MR settings. The majority of these were in residential settings with 6 or fewer beds.

67. This is an estimate of state Medicaid matching funds based on the average federal match across states in 1992 (58 percent) and the total state funds spent on MR/DD services. The actual state/federal split would vary across states.

68. We would like to acknowledge the contributions to the writing of this section made by Dr. Ronald Conley.

69. Kimberly Hoagwood and Agnes Rupp, "Mental Health Service Needs, Use, and Costs for Children and Adolescents with Mental Disorders and their Families: Preliminary Evidence," in Center for Mental Health Services, *Mental Health, United States, 1994*, R.W. Manderscheid and M.A. Sonnenchien (eds.), DHHS Pub. No. (SMA) 94-3000, Washington, D.C., 1994.

70. For a brief review of children's use of mental health services see Kimberly Hoagwood and Agnes Rupp, "Mental Health Service Needs, Use, and Costs for Children and Adolescents with Mental Disorders and their Families: Preliminary Evidence," in Center for Mental Health Services, *Mental Health, United States, 1994*, R.W. Manderscheid and M.A. Sonnenchien (eds.), DHHS Pub. No. (SMA) 94-3000, Washington, D.C., 1994.

71. This information is based on David Braddock, "Community Mental Health and Mental Retardation Services in the United States: A Comparative Study of Resource Allocation," *The American Journal of Psychiatry*, Vol. 149, No. 2, February 1992.

72. Information on total spending is from Theodore Lutterman and Vera Hollen, "Change in State Mental Health Agency Revenues and Expenditures Between Fiscal Years 1981 and 1990," in Center for Mental Health Services and the National Institute of Mental Health, *Mental Health, United States, 1992*, R.W. Manderscheid and M.A. Sonnenchien (eds.), DHHS Pub. No. (SMA) 92-1942, Washington, D.C., 1992. Information for children is taken from Theodore Lutterman, Vera Hollen, and Michael Hogan, "Funding Sources and Expenditures of State Mental Health Agencies: Revenue/Expenditure Study Results Fiscal Year 1990," National Association of State Mental Health Program Directors Research Institute, March 1993.

73. For a more general discussion of the differential growth in community-based services for mental health and MR/DD services, see David Braddock, "Community Mental Health and Mental Retardation Services in the United States: A Comparative Study of Resource Allocation," *The American Journal of Psychiatry*, Vol. 149, No. 2, February 1992.

74. The Head Start program has established specific diagnostic criteria for children with disabilities. To be counted as disabled in Head Start, children must be professionally diagnosed as having one of several disabling conditions and because of this condition, require special education and related services. Disabling conditions are blindness, visual impairment/disability, deafness, hearing impairment/disability, physical disability (orthopedic disability), speech impairment (communication disorder), health impairment, mental retardation, serious emotional disturbance, or specific learning disabilities. Children must be diagnosed by "appropriate professionals who work with children with these conditions and have certification and/or licensure to make these diagnoses."

75. U.S. Department of Health and Human Services, "Status of Children with Disabilities in Head Start Programs," Eighteenth Annual Report of the U.S. Department of Health and Human Services to the Congress of the United States on Services Provided

to Children with Disabilities in the Head Start Program, U.S. Department of Health and Human Services, Administration for Children and Families, Head Start Bureau, 1992.

76. Valerie Bradley, James Knoll, and John Agosta, *Emerging Issues in Family Support*, AAMR Monographs, 1992. This entire section is based on the authors' analysis of their survey of state family support programs in 1989.

77. This discussion is based on the taxonomy of family support services found in Valerie Bradley, James Knoll, and John Agosta, *Emerging Issues in Family Support*, AAMR Monographs, 1992, Table 4.

78. David Braddock, Richard Hemp, Lynn Bachelder, and Glenn Fujiura, *The State of the States in Developmental Disabilities*, Institute on Disability and Human Development, The University of Illinois at Chicago, October 1994.

APPENDIXES

SOURCES OF NATIONAL DATA ON CHILDREN WITH DISABILITIES

Publicly funded nationally representative surveys are important sources of information on children with disabilities. Although not geared to collecting data on children with disability specifically, two of the most useful surveys for this purpose are the Survey of Income and Program Participation and the National Health Interview Survey.

THE SURVEY OF INCOME AND PROGRAM PARTICIPATION

The Survey of Income and Program Participation (SIPP) is based on a nationally representative sample of households from the civilian non-institutional population, and tracks groups (or panels) of individuals and their households for approximately two and a half years. The first panel was initiated in October 1983 (the 1984 panel) with adults (persons aged 15 and over) in approximately 20,000 households.[1] The second and subsequent panels begin in February of each calendar year, and participants are interviewed every four months (each called a "wave") over the two and one-half year life of the panel.

In addition to the main SIPP questionnaire, the third wave of the 1984 panel was asked a battery of disability questions. More recently, disability supplements were given to the third and sixth waves of the 1990 panel and the third wave of the 1991 panel.[2] The data from these two samples combined cover approximately 30,000 interviewed households. Information about the disability status of children was obtained by interviewing the parents or guardians of children under the age of 22.

SIPP-derived estimates of the prevalence of disabilities in the child population are shown in Tables A-1 and A-2. The disability questions in SIPP differed by the child's age. Parents with a child under age six,

Table A-1 DISABILITY STATUS OF CHILDREN 0 TO 17 YEARS OLD,
BY AGE AND SEX: 1991–92

Age:	All Children		Males		Females	
	Percent with a:		Percent with a:		Percent with a:	
	Disability	Severe Disability	Disability	Severe Disability	Disability	Severe Disability
Under 3 years	2.2	0.4	2.2	0.5	2.1	0.1
3 to 5 years	5.2	0.7	6.2	0.9	4.1	0.4
6 to 14 years	6.3	1.3	8.2	1.5	4.3	1.0
15 to 17 years	9.3	3.1	10.8	3.1	7.7	3.1
Total Under 18	5.8	1.3	7.2	1.5	4.4	1.1

Source of Data: 1990 and 1991 SIPP.
Source: John M. McNeil, *Americans with Disabilities: 1991–92*, U.S. Bureau of the Census, Current Population Reports, P70-33, U.S. Government Printing Office, Washington, D.C., 1993.

for example, were asked if their child "had any limitations at all in the usual kind of activities done by most children their age" (because of a physical, learning, or mental health condition) and if their child had received therapy or diagnostic services designed to meet his/her developmental needs. Parents of all children aged 6 to 21 were asked if their child had any limitations in their ability to do regular schoolwork. For children aged 3 to 14, parents were also asked if their child had a "long lasting condition that limited their ability to walk, run, or use stairs." Finally, children age 15 and older were also asked the standard set of questions on limitations of activity developed for adult SIPP respondents. The functional activities covered in the survey include seeing, hearing, having one's speech understood, lifting and carrying, walking up a flight of stairs, and walking.

Children were classified as having a *severe* disability if they: (a) used a wheelchair or had used another special aid for 6 months or longer; (b) were unable to perform one or more functional activities or needed assistance with an activity of daily living (ADL) or an instrumental activity of daily living (IADL);[3] (c) were prevented from working at a job or doing housework; or (d) had a selected condition including autism, cerebral palsy, or mental retardation. Also, children receiving SSI were considered to have a severe disability.[4]

The 1991 SIPP data indicate that around 6 percent of all children under the age of 17 have a disability (see Table A-1). The proportion of children identified as having a disability (and the proportion identified as having a severe disability) increases dramatically with the age of the child. Furthermore, as children age, the proportion of boys

Table A-2 DISABILITY STATUS OF CHILDREN 0 TO 17 YEARS OLD: 1991–92

	Number (thousands)	Percent
Children less than 3 years	11,791	100.0
With a disability	254	2.2
Limited in usual kind of activities	149	1.3
Received services for developmental needs	183	1.6
With a severe disability	41	0.4
Children 3 to 5 years	11,511	100.0
With a disability	597	5.2
Limited in usual kind of activities	294	2.6
Received services for developmental needs	498	4.3
Limited in ability to walk, run, or use stairs	147	1.3
With a severe disability	75	0.7
Children 6 to 14 years	32,766	100.0
With a disability	2,062	6.3
Limited in ability to do regular school work	1,764	5.4
Limited in ability to walk, run, or use stairs	524	1.6
With a severe disability	412	1.3
Children 15 to 17 years	10,067	100.0
With a disability	933	9.3
Limited in ability to do regular school work	438	4.4
With a severe disability	309	3.1
All Children Under 18 years	66,135	100.0
With a disability	3,846	5.8
With a severe disability	837	1.3

Source of Data: 1990 and 1991 SIPP.
Source: John M. McNeil, *Americans with Disabilities: 1991–92*, U.S. Bureau of the Census, Current Population Reports, P70-33, U.S. Government Printing Office, Washington, D.C., 1993.

with a disability increasingly exceeds the corresponding proportion for girls of the same age. Thus, while the percentage of children under three with a disability is virtually the same for boys and girls (just over 2 percent), by the time they reach age 15 to 17, close to 11 percent of boys are reported to have a disability, compared to less then 8 percent of girls. The most common conditions identified as the cause of a child's disability are shown in Table A-3.

THE NATIONAL HEALTH INTERVIEW SURVEY

A second important source of information on children's health is the National Health Interview Survey (NHIS), conducted for the National

Table A-3 CONDITIONS REPORTED AS CAUSE OF DISABILITY,
CHILDREN 0 TO 17 YEARS OLD: 1991–92

Condition (first, second, or third condition)	Number	Percent Distribution
TOTAL	4,858	100.0
Asthma	311	6.4
Autism	48	1.0
Blindness or vision problems	144	3.0
Cancer	26	0.5
Cerebral Palsy	129	2.7
Deafness or serious trouble hearing	116	2.4
Diabetes	14	0.3
Drug or alcohol problem or disorder	48	1.0
Epilepsy or seizure disorder	128	2.6
Hay fever or other respiratory allergies	76	1.6
Head or spinal cord injury	45	0.9
Heart trouble	44	0.9
Impairment or deformity of back, side, foot, or leg	121	2.5
Impairment or deformity of finger, hand, or arm	27	0.6
Learning disability	1,435	29.5
Mental or emotional problem or disorder	305	6.3
Mental retardation	331	6.8
Missing legs, feet, toes, arms, hands, or fingers	70	1.4
Paralysis of any kind	73	1.5
Speech problems	634	13.1
Tonsillitis or repeated ear infections	80	1.6
Other	653	13.4

Note: Table figures refer to conditions, not children. A child may have more than one of the conditions listed.
Source of Data: 1990 and 1991 SIPP.
Source: John M. McNeil, Americans with Disabilities: 1991–92, U.S. Bureau of the Census, Current Population Reports, P70-33, U.S. Government Printing Office, Washington, D.C., 1993.

Center for Health Statistics by the U.S. Bureau of the Census. The NHIS is an on-going household survey based on a sample designed to represent the noninstitutionalized civilian population. In 1988 and earlier in 1981, the NHIS included a special supplement on child health. In each surveyed household, one child was selected at random as the subject of the child health supplemental questionnaire. For the 1988 NHIS, data were collected for 17,110 children under the age of 18.[5]

The checklist of conditions included in the NHIS fall into the following general categories: (1) blindness and other trouble seeing, (2) missing extremities, (3) permanent impairment, stiffness, deformity,

(4) cerebral palsy, (5) diabetes, (6) sickle cell disease, (7) asthma, (8) other respiratory allergy, hay fever, (9) eczema and skin allergies, (10) epilepsy or convulsions without fever, (11) arthritis or other joint problem, (12) heart disease, and (13) digestive allergies. Parents are read an extensive list of conditions (in lay terminology) and are asked if the sample child had any of them during the preceding 12 months.[6] These results provide estimates of *annual* prevalence. Not surprisingly, including or excluding children with conditions such as hay fever, acne, or repaired congenital defects greatly affects the estimated total number of children with a chronic condition. Drawing on the 1988 NHIS alone, various studies estimate the proportion of American children with one or more chronic conditions to range from around 5 percent to more than 30 percent (see Table A-4). As the second and third columns of Table A-4 indicate, the majority of children with a chronic illness have only a minor condition (such as a mild allergy or skin conditions) that is not likely to result in any type of disability or activity limitation. The NHIS data suggest that around 5 percent of children have a chronic condition that is disabling. More recent results from the 1993 NHIS indicate that 4.4 million children under the age of 18, or 6.6 percent of all children in this age group, are reported to have some degree of limitation of activity.[7]

In addition to chronic conditions, the 1988 NHIS Child Health supplement asked of parents whether their child had *ever had* (1) a delay in growth or development, (2) a learning disability, and (3) an emotional or behavioral problem that lasted three months or more. In general, there are few nationally representative sources of information on these conditions. This NHIS question provides an estimate of lifetime prevalence and reveals that almost 20 percent of children aged 3 to 17 have one of these conditions at some point in time. When younger children with developmental delays are included, the number of affected children is about 10.7 million.[8]

An important supplement to the National Health Interview Survey—known as the 1994/95 Disability Survey—is currently being conducted. This survey represents the most comprehensive and coordinated effort to date to collect national data on disability. The survey was designed to provide information on several priority areas, including the Americans with Disabilities Act goals and the extent of disability among children.[9] The 1994/95 Disability Survey actually evolved out of four other more specialized surveys including the National Child Health Assessment and Planning Project funded by the Maternal and Child Health Bureau and devoted exclusively to children.

Table A-4 PREVALENCE OF CHILDREN WITH CHRONIC HEALTH CONDITIONS: RESULTS FROM THE NATIONAL HEALTH INTERVIEW SURVEY

Source:	Severe	Moderate	Mild	Total	Survey	N	Population
1. Newacheck & Stoddard, 1994	1%	3%	15%	19%	NHIS, 1988	17,110	< 18
2. Newacheck & Taylor, 1992	2%	9%	20%	31%	NHIS, 1988	17,110	< 18
3. Newacheck et al., 1991	3%	7%	21%	32%	NHIS, 1988	7,465	10–17
4. Gortmaker et al., 1990				9%	NHIS, 1981	11,699	4–17
5. Newacheck, 1989	.5%	4%	2%	6%	NHIS, 1988	15,181	10–17

Comments:

1. Defined chronic conditions as one of 17 condition groups listed in the NHIS (the checklist method). Levels of severity correspond to 1, 2, or 3 or more conditions.
2. Defined chronic conditions as one of 19 condition groups listed in the NHIS (the checklist method). Defined severity as extent of "bother" and degree of limitation in daily activities.
3. Defined chronic conditions as one of 19 condition groups listed in the NHIS (the checklist method). Levels of severity correspond to 1, 2, or 3 or more conditions.
4. Defined chronic conditions using checklist method.
5. Defined population as limited in activities. Mild is limited in nonmajor activities; moderate is limited in kind or amount of major activity; severe is unable to conduct major activity.

Sources:

Henry T. Ireys and Susan Shapiro Gross, "Curriculum on Children with Special Health Care Needs and Their Families," Department of Maternal and Child Health, School of Hygiene and Public Health, The Johns Hopkins University, Baltimore, MD, April 1994.

Paul W. Newacheck and Jeffrey J. Stoddard, "Prevalence and Impact of Multiple Childhood Chronic Illnesses," Journal of Pediatrics, Vol. 124, No. 1, January 1994.

The 1994/95 Disability Survey consists of two parts. The first follows the annual NHIS core interview for 1994/95 and covers all households in the NHIS sample. This portion of the survey will provide information on the prevalence of disability in the country and will help identify four sub-populations of particular policy interest (persons with mental retardation and/or developmental disabilities; persons who are actual or potential SSI recipients; working-age adults who are actual or potential Social Security Disability Insurance (SSDI) recipients; and children). The second phase of data collection will occur about 6 to 9 months following the first interview. Data will be collected from those identified in the first phase and will focus on service use and expenditure patterns. It is expected that during the two years of data collection, information will be gathered for approximately 120,000 individuals (residing in 240,000 households) in Phase I and approximately 40,000 individuals in Phase II. Preliminary results from this important source of information on persons with disabilities are not expected until 1996.

Notes

1. Other than the 1990 panel which also consisted of 20,000 households, the sample size of all subsequent panels of SIPP has been 12,000 households.

2. These waves were completed during the last three months of 1991 and the first month of 1992.

3. ADLs covered by SIPP include getting around inside the home, getting in or out of bed or a chair, bathing, dressing, eating, and toileting. IADLs include going outside the home, keeping track of money or bills, preparing meals, doing light housework, and using the telephone.

4. SIPP can only identify child SSI recipients age 15 and older.

5. In approximately 90 percent of these cases the survey respondent was the child's parent (usually the mother). The National Center for Health Statistics is lowering the age for self-reporting data for the NHIS from 17 to 12 years.

6. It is also important to note that because parents underreport cancers and mental health problems (without physical manifestations), the 1988 NHIS did not include these in their condition lists.

7. V. Benson and M.A. Marano, *Current Estimates from the National Health Interview Survey, 1993*, National Center for Health Statistics, Vital Health Statistics, Series 10, No. 190, December 1994.

8. N. Zill and C.A. Schoenborn, *Developmental, Learning, and Emotional Problems: Health of Our Nation's Children, United States, 1988,* Advance Data from Vital and Health Statistics, No. 190, National Center for Health Statistics, Hyattsville, MD, 1990.

9. Michele Adler, "Federal Disability Data: Creating a Structure in the 1990s to Further the Goals of the ADA," presented at the National Council on Disability Conference, Furthering the Goals of the ADA through Disability Policy Research in the 1990s, Washington, D.C., 1992.

PRIVATE EXPENDITURES ON CHILDREN WITH DISABILITIES

Expenditures on public programs serving children with disabilities represent only that portion of the total costs borne by taxpayers in general. In addition, there are many direct and indirect costs incurred by families. Public and private costs, however, are interrelated. Understanding the private costs of caring for children with disabilities, and how these costs are distributed, is an important part of understanding how the system of programs available to families functions.

It is beyond the scope of this study to do a full review of the literature on the private costs of caring for children with disabilities. However, we include this summary on this important topic to provide some context for our discussion of public expenditures. We first review some of the research on the medical costs to families of children with disabilities and then discuss additional non-medical private costs.

Children with disabling chronic conditions have greater medical and social service usage than other children. Drawing on analyses of the 1980 National Medical Care Utilization and Expenditure Survey (NMCUES), Newacheck and McManus found that disabled children are three times more likely to be hospitalized than nondisabled children, and once hospitalized, stay twice as long as children who do not have a disability.[10] As a result of these differences, children with chronic disabling conditions (approximately 5 percent of all children) account for almost one-third of all hospital days among children under the age of 18. The most severely disabled children (who are unable to attend school or to engage in ordinary activities such as play) spend 40 times more days in the hospital than their nondisabled counterparts.

Not surprisingly, children with disabilities average more physician contacts annually (11 compared to fewer than 4 among nondisabled children) and use nonphysician professional services such as physical therapists, nurses, and psychologists, six times more frequently than children who do not have a disability. They also require twice the number of prescription medications and are at least twice as likely to need some type of assistive aids such as vision and hearing devices, orthopedic aids, and medical transportation services. Newacheck and McManus estimate that, overall, children with disabilities use twice as many health services as nondisabled children. The difference is even larger for inpatient hospital and nonphysician professional services. Reliable national estimates for other health-related needs such as durable medical equipment, home renovation, expendable medical supplies, and institutional care are not available.

These differences in hospital stays, physician and nonphysician contacts, and prescribed medications translate into large differentials in medical charges and family out-of-pocket expenditures. As Table B-1 illustrates, total average annual charges for health services were almost three times higher for children with a disability ($760 compared to $263 for other children in 1980 dollars). This large differential is found in each of the five specific cost categories reported in Table B-1. Out-of-pocket expenses paid directly by the family are also shown in the table. Out-of-pocket expenses among families of children with disabilities were about twice as high as those among other families. Overall, out-of-pocket expenses for children with a disability accounted for 18 percent of total medical charges. Because third-party insurance coverage tends to cover a greater share of hospital-based care, out-of-pocket expenses ranged from 7 percent for inpatient hospital charges to 59 percent of prescription medical charges.

Newacheck and McManus' analysis of NMCUES data also shows that medical charge and out-of-pocket expenses are not distributed evenly across families with disabled children. The 10 percent of families with the lowest total charges and out-of-pocket expenses incurred almost no charges or expenses. By contrast, the top 10 percent of families experienced total charges of $1,800 or more in 1980 dollars (or 65 percent of all charges accumulated). Out-of-pocket expenses were similarly skewed: one-quarter of these families had almost no out-of-pocket expenses, whereas the top ten percent of families paid over $300 in 1980 dollars. In comparing disabled children and youth with high and low out-of-pocket expenses, Newacheck and McManus find that:

> ... disabled children with high direct expenses were likely to be older. By comparison to persons with low out-of-pocket expenses, those with high expenses were also disproportionately girls and white. In contrast to the pattern for total charges, low income persons were disproportionately represented in the low out-of-pocket expense group. That is,

Table B-1 AVERAGE CHARGES AND OUT-OF-POCKET EXPENSES IN 1980 DOLLARS FOR PERSONS LESS THAN 21 YEARS OF AGE, 1980 MICRODATA FROM THE NATIONAL CENTER FOR HEALTH STATISTICS

	Total ($)	Hospital Inpatient Services ($)	Physician Services ($)	Nonphysician Services ($)	Prescribed Medications ($)	Other Medical Expenses ($)
Charges						
Limited in Activity	760	344	256	112	29	20
Not Limited in Activity	263	123	103	17	12	8
Out-of-Pocket Expenses						
Limited in Activity	135	23	70	16	17	10
Not Limited in Activity	76	16	40	7	8	6

Source: Paul W. Newacheck and Margaret McManus, "Financing Health Care for Disabled Children," Pediatrics, Vol. 81, No. 3, March 1988.

low income disabled children tended to be at the high end of the total charge distribution but at the low end of the out-of-pocket expenses distribution. In part, this phenomenon can be attributed to Medicaid which tends to have minimal or nonexistent copayment levels when compared to other third-party payors. Nevertheless, approximately 15 percent of the high out-of-pocket expense group had family incomes that placed them below the official poverty line.[11]

In short, Newacheck and McManus' analyses indicate that the families of children with disabilities do indeed bear higher medical costs and out-of-pocket expenses than other families whose children are not limited in activity. Furthermore, the magnitude of these additional medical expenses varies considerably among the families of interest. Finally, because many of the services used primarily by children with disabilities were not included in the NMCUES data, existing estimates may fall short of the true differences in medical costs and expenditures made by families with and without children with disabilities. One attempt to inventory the many medical and related costs incurred by families in caring for children with chronic illnesses is reproduced in Table B-2.

It is important to recognize that medical costs and related expenditures are only one type of cost associated with caring for a child with a disability. Other important costs include psycho-social costs. Among financial costs, among the largest are indirect costs such as forgone earnings or loss of other financial opportunities. Unfortunately, there are few reliable (and generalizable) estimates of exactly how high these types of costs are.[12] Some general observations, however, can be made. The burden of caring for children is carried disproportionately by mothers, and is likely to restrict their extra-domestic activities. The direct and indirect costs of caring for a disabled child are also likely to vary with the income of the family. As Hobbs, Perrin, and Ireys observe:

> Overall, a childhood chronic illness has a different impact on income for different socioeconomic groups. For families in poverty, and especially for single-parent families, the presence of a child with a chronic illness may effectively remove any opportunity to earn sufficient money to climb out of poverty. Real income loss is small because income is small in total dollars; opportunity for increasing income, however, may vanish under the demands for care. For families in middle- or upper-income brackets, the accumulated costs of care not covered by insurance together with income unearned take an ever-increasing toll.[13]

Table B-2 SOURCES OF COST IN THE CARE OF CHRONICALLY ILL CHILDREN

Initial Identification or Evaluation Period	Initial Treatment	Continuing Treatment	Special Services Needed for Limited Duration	Daily Care Routine Services
Emergency room services	Hospitalization	Physician or clinic visits	Camp	Medications
Physician visits	Physician visits in hospital	Urine and blood tests	Respite care	Injections
Urine and blood tests	Outpatient physician visits	Physical therapy	Individual or family counseling	Bowel and bladder hygiene
Hospitalization	Urine and blood tests	Home nursing services	Specialty care for complications	Care of personal appearance
Neurological tests	Teaching parent/family about the disease	Psychological tests	Re-education in management of care	Appliance care
Transportation	Physical therapy	Dental evaluation	Genetic counseling	Home health nurse visits
Phone calls	Dental visits	Orthopedic fittings	Infant stimulation	Special foods
Intensive care unit services	Orthopedic fittings	General pediatric care for common health problems	Parent support group	Physical therapy
Assessment of family's functioning	Financial evaluation	Transportation	Homemaker services	
Psychological or developmental testing	Transportation	Phone calls	Home health nurse	
	Phone calls	Surgery and operating room procedures	Transportation	
	Intensive care unit services	Insurance premiums, deductibles, and copayments	Special clothes	
	Social work services	Monitoring of family functioning	Remodeling of house	
	Surgery		Child care for siblings during visit to clinic or hospital	
	Room/board during extended hospital stays		Special foods	
			Relocation	
			Home respirators	
			Emergency room care	
			Occupational therapy and vocational training	

Source: "Defining the Costs of Care," Chapter 6 in Nicholas Hobbs, James M. Perrin, and Henry T. Ireys, *Chronically Ill Children and Their Families: Problems, Prospects, and Proposals from the Vanderbilt Study,* Jossey-Bass, 1985, p. 174.

For the families of children who are severely disabled, however, the burden of family care "transcends urban and rural boundaries, household size, and income levels."[14] Interestingly, Leonard, Brust, and Sapienza, in their analysis of data on severely disabled children applying to the Services for Children with Handicaps (SCH) program in Minnesota in 1988, also found that monthly out-of-pocket expenses and time spent caring for the child were positively correlated. When they analyzed the determinants of time spent daily caring for a child, they concluded that "the opportunity cost of caring for a child who suffers from a more severe disease or disabling condition is driving the greater financial burden of the[se] families." This opportunity cost includes the earnings a family caregiver is forgoing by not working in the paid labor market as well as the value of other activities that could be undertaken in that time.

Empirical estimates of the full costs of caring for chronically ill and disabled children are incomplete and difficult to assess. After attempting to compare six studies of the caregiving costs of families raising chronically ill and handicapped children, Jacobs and McDermott concluded that a major problem was "the lack of uniformity among the studies with regard to categories of costs, survey methods, and variables used to explain cost variations."[15] Similar conclusions have been reached by many others interested in understanding the costs of raising a child with a disability. Despite these limitations, below we review the studies examined by Jacobs and McDermott.

Jacobs and McDermott propose classifying family costs into four categories: (1) direct, out-of-pocket home costs on recurring items, such as adaptive aids, child care, special clothing, telephone, etc.; (2) travel costs related to the child's condition, including direct costs such as automobile fuel and maintenance and (if not included in another category) the indirect costs of time spent transporting the child; (3) costs for durable equipment such as wheelchairs and braces, and home renovation; and (4) indirect costs (including forgone earnings and leisure time) associated with caregiving, transportation, and other functions.

The six studies examined by Jacobs and McDermott are summarized in Table B-3. The studies examined employed different methodologies, covering different time periods at different points in the year (ideally, annual cost estimates should cover both the school year and summer months).[16] One study (by Houts) included both children and adults but did not report estimates separately for the two groups. The final line in Table B-3 takes forgone earnings into account by including the value of lost earnings in both the numerator (total costs) and the

Table B-3 CHARACTERISTICS OF DATA PROVIDED BY SIX STUDIES OF FINANCIAL BURDEN TO CAREGIVING FAMILIES

Characteristics	Gordon (1978)	Lansky (1979)	Bloom (1985)	Houts (1984)	Bodkin (1982)	McCollum (1971)
Disease Considered	Spina Bifida	Cancer	Cancer	Cancer	Cancer	Cystic Fibrosis
Number of Patients Observed	702	70	589	139	59	62
Time Period Observed	7.5 years	1 week–3 mos.	1 week, May–Oct.	3 weeks	1 week, NS	1 year
Costs Included:						
Direct Home	Yes	Yes	Yes	Yes	Yes	Yes
Direct Travel	No	Yes	Yes	Yes	NS	Yes
Durable Equipment	Yes	No	No	No	Yes	Yes
Time Cost	No	Yes, 0	Yes, 0	Yes	No, 0	No
Annual Money Cost	...	$3,324	$4,012	$1,121	...	$334
Annual Time Cost	...	$1,924	$4,697	$1,514	...	...
Money Cost Divided by Money Income	...	14 percent	15 percent	...	...	...
Total Cost Divided by Full Income	...	15 percent	28 percent	...	20 percent	...

Note: Under costs included, Yes indicates that the cost category was included in the study; No indicates it was not. 0 indicates that the cost category was included, but was placed in another cost category in that particular study. NS indicates not specified.

Source: Philip Jacobs and Suzanne McDermott, "Family Caregiver Costs of Chronically Ill and Handicapped Children: Method and Literature Review," Public Health Reports, Vol. 104, No. 2, March–April 1989, pp. 158–163.

168   *Serving Children with Disabilities*

denominator (potential or full earnings). None of the original studies examined full or potential earnings but the reviewers calculated these when sufficient information was available.

Childhood cancer was the most common illness examined. The two U.S. cancer studies (Lansky and Bloom) show quite similar money costs (between $3,000 and $4,000 annually). The estimated time costs are very different, however, with Bloom's estimate more than twice as high as that of Lansky. This may result from differences in the time periods covered and the functions considered (e.g., Bloom only looked at costs associated with accompanying a child to the hospital while Lansky examined time losses from all illness-related functions). Despite these cross-study differences, the general theme to emerge from the cancer studies is that cancer takes a substantial financial toll on families. Bodkin's United Kingdom study indicates that this is not limited to American families.

In summary, the limited evidence regarding private family costs associated with raising a child with a disability indicates that these costs are significant and vary across many dimensions, including type of disability, family, and community, as well as over time for the same family. Costs are not only economic, but emotional and social. The availability of resources and services through the public sector for families of children with disabilities will affect the direct and indirect private costs the family bears and ultimately the well-being of these children.

Notes

10. See Paul W. Newacheck and Margaret McManus, "Financing Health Care for Disabled Children," *Pediatrics*, Vol. 81, No. 3, March 1988, and Paul W. Newacheck, "Financing the Health Care of Children with Chronic Illnesses," *Pediatric Annals*, Vol. 19, No. 1, January 1990.

11. Paul W. Newacheck and Margaret McManus, "Financing Health Care for Disabled Children," *Pediatrics*, Vol. 81, No. 3, March 1988, p. 390.

12. For a review of some of the more theoretical and methodological issues associated with measuring these types of costs, see Thomas A. Hodgson and Mark R. Meiners, "Cost-of-Illness Methodology: A Guide to Current Practices and Procedures," *Health and Society*, Vol. 60, No. 3, 1982.

13. "Defining the Costs of Care," Chapter 6 in Nicholas Hobbs, James M. Perrin, and Henry T. Ireys, *Chronically Ill Children and Their Families: Problems, Prospects, and Proposals from the Vanderbilt Study*, Jossey-Bass, 1985, p. 184.

14. Barbara Leonard, Janny Dwyer Brust, and James J. Sapienza, "Financial and Time Costs to Parents of Severely Disabled Children," *Public Health Reports*, Vol. 107, No. 3, May–June 1992, p. 151.

15. Philip Jacobs and Suzanne McDermott, "Family Caregiver Costs of Chronically Ill and Handicapped Children: Method and Literature Review," *Public Health Reports*, Vol. 104, No. 2, March–April 1989.

16. As the authors correctly point out, family costs are likely to vary significantly from one family to another. Because costs are likely to vary over time (both in relation to the age of the child and to years since the onset of the illness/injury), it is also important to examine cost-time profiles.

INTERNATIONAL PERSPECTIVES ON CHILDREN WITH DISABILITIES[17]

Governments around the world attempt in various ways to meet the needs of children with disabilities. Examining child disability systems in other countries, therefore, should provide insight and perspective on our own system. Unfortunately, the literature comparing services and supports for children with disabilities across countries is somewhat limited. A conference held in 1988 entitled "A Cross-Cultural Conference on Supports for Families with a Child with a Disability," however, provides some perspective on how child disability issues are approached in other countries. Common developments and trends identified were:

- A growing sense that persons with disabilities can and should live in the community and not in institutional settings;
- The growth of national legislation to provide increased services to persons with disabilities, especially children;
- The development of rights-based guarantees, both to persons with disabilities and (to a lesser extent) to their families, of participation in decisions affecting them;
- The belief that the environment, physical and social, is the key factor that determines the extent to which an individual's impairment becomes a handicap;
- A recognition that the family, in both the attitudes it has and the support it receives, is the central social institution affecting the life of the child with disabilities; and
- Increasing development of organizations among persons with disabilities, parents of children with disabilities, and other interested groups, including professionals; there is, however, generally little in the way of collaboration among these groups.[18]

PREVALENCE RATES OF CHILDREN WITH DISABILITIES

The United Nations maintains a database containing prevalence rates of children with disabilities for many countries.[19] The disability rates are derived from national surveys and censuses from the years 1975–1984. Unfortunately, comparing the prevalence rates of children with disabilities from the different national surveys is highly problematic because the surveys often use different definitions of disability and cover different population groups.

In defining disability, the surveys are divided between those that use functional measures and those that use categorical measures. Also, there is variation within the two major types of definitions as well. Categorical definitions vary depending upon which impairments are included in the definition. Functional definitions vary by which activities an able-bodied person should be able to perform.

Comparing the disability rates is further complicated by variation in the population groups covered by the surveys. The surveys cover different segments of the child population. Some surveys cover all children while others cover only older children, younger children, urban children, rural children, children not attending school, etc. If disability rates differ for these groups then one cannot compare surveys that cover different populations.

Table C-1, nonetheless, summarizes national surveys on the prevalence rates of children with disabilities in selected countries. The surveys are from various years between 1975 and 1984. The disability rates are for children under age fifteen except when noted. The definition of disability is listed when known. The most striking aspect of the table is the great variation in disability rates. The rates range from 1.1 per thousand in Burma to 56.7 per thousand in Canada. For two of the three countries that have multiple surveys there is great variation in the disability rates derived from the surveys. The two Thailand surveys yield rates of 5.5 per thousand for one and 35.5 per thousand for the other. The two Ethiopian surveys yield rates of 20.9 per thousand for one and 2.0 per thousand for the other. The variation of disability rates within Thailand and Ethiopia and the great variation of disability rates across national surveys strongly support the argument made above, that comparing the national surveys is tenuous at best.

Disability rates appear very high for two developed countries: Canada and Austria. Canada has the highest disability rate in the table at 56.7 per thousand and Austria has the third highest rate at 32.3 per

Table C-1 DISABILITY PREVALENCE RATES AMONG CHILDREN UNDER AGE 15 PER 1,000 CHILDREN UNDER AGE 15, SELECTED COUNTRIES

Country	Year	Disability Rate	Definition of Disability (if available)	Age Group (if different than under age 15)
Cape Verde	1980	4.2	Incapacitated	10–14
Comoros	1980	8.6		
Egypt	1976	1.3		
Ethiopia	1979–81	20.9		
Ethiopia	1981	2.0		
Mali	1976	6.8		
Tunisia	1975	2.7		
Tunisia	1984	2.7		
Bahrain	1981	4.3		
Burma	1983	1.1	Economically Inactive	10–14
China	1983	14.4		
Kuwait	1980	3.7		
Pakistan	1981	2.0		
Philippines	1980	23.8	Impaired	
Thailand	1981	5.5		
Thailand	1983	35.5	Not in School	6–14
Turkey	1975	10.1		
Austria	1976	32.3		
Canada	1983	56.7		
Mexico	1980	27.5	Not in School	6–14
Netherlands Antilles	1981	17.7		
Venezuela	1981	5.5	Economically Inactive	12–14
Fiji	1982	2.5	Economically Inactive	

Source: United Nations Statistical Office. United Nations Disability Statistics Microcomputer Data Base (DISTAT1), Version 1, Series Number 00201.0-0-01007, DTAB6. New York: United Nations, 1988.

thousand. This might be due to the use of a functional definition of disability as opposed to a categorical definition, more advanced survey techniques, and/or cultural differences in how disability is viewed and recognized.[20]

The conclusion from examining the data available on the prevalence rates of children with disabilities across several countries is that a more standardized method of measuring disability rates is needed. The international community needs to agree upon a definition of disability, a common denominator for calculating disability rates, and a survey coverage population, before useful international comparisons of disability rates can be made. Even then, it may be difficult to determine if survey techniques are common.

PROGRAMS FOR CHILDREN WITH DISABILITIES

Examining the government-provided services and supports available to children with disabilities in selected countries provides some insight into relative availability of supports across countries. Table C-2 summarizes the public programs for children with disabilities in nine countries: Australia, Canada, Israel, Japan, Kenya, Sweden, the United Kingdom, the United States, and Uruguay. The list of countries examined here is not meant to be exhaustive. Programs are divided into four categories: rehabilitative services and/or special equipment, special education, income maintenance, and medical care.

Rehabilitative services and/or special equipment include services such as diagnostic assessment, personal and vocational adjustment services, training in activities of daily living, adaptive equipment such as electric wheelchairs, and home modifications such as ramps or wider doorways. Rehabilitative services and equipment are available in most of the countries. Australia, Canada, Israel, Japan, Sweden, the United Kingdom, and even Kenya, which does not have a national welfare system, provide some sort of rehabilitative services or special equipment.

All of the countries provide special education programs, except for Kenya where public education is not provided in many rural areas (despite legislative provisions for universal education). In most of the countries there is a movement towards integrating children with disabilities into ordinary schools. Canada, Israel, Japan, Sweden, the United States, and Uruguay educate at least some children with dis-

Table C-2 GOVERNMENT-PROVIDED SERVICES AND SUPPORTS FOR FAMILIES
WITH DISABLED CHILDREN, SELECTED COUNTRIES

Country	Rehabilitative Services/Special Equipment	Special Education	Income Maintenance	Medical Care
Australia	Yes	Yes	Yes	Universal health insurance
Canada	Yes	Yes	Yes[a]	Universal health insurance
Israel	Yes	Yes	Yes	
Japan	Yes	Yes	Means tested[b]	Universal health insurance[c]
Kenya				
Sweden	Yes	Yes	Yes	Universal health insurance
United Kingdom	Yes	Yes	Yes	Universal health insurance
United States		Yes	Means tested	Means tested medical benefits
Uruguay		Yes	Yes	Universal health insurance

a. Only in certain provinces.
b. Japan also allows tax deductions for families with children with disabilities which are not means tested.
c. Medical expenses not covered by insurance are subsidized.
Source: Alan Gartner, Dorothy Kerzner Lipsky, and Ann P. Turnbull, 1991. *Supporting Families with a Child with a Disability: An International Outlook*, Baltimore: Paul H. Brookes, 1991, Chapters 4 and 6, and Social Security Administration, 1994, *Social Security Programs Throughout the World—1993*, p. xxxiii–xxxvii.

abilities in ordinary schools, although many children with disabilities are still separated from their peers.

Nearly all of the countries listed provide income maintenance to families with children with disabilities as well. Kenya is the only exception.[21] What is more, most of the countries provide benefits regardless of family income. Only the United States and Japan have an income criteria for benefits. Cash support programs for families with children with disabilities are consistent with the trend away from institutionalization, because parents can better afford to care for their children at home as opposed to committing them to government subsidized institutions.

Two-thirds of the countries provide subsidized medical care to at least some children with disabilities. Australia, Canada, Japan, Sweden, and the United Kingdom provide medical care via universal health insurance. The United States provides health insurance only to some low-income children. Japan supplements health insurance for children with disabilities by subsidizing medical expenses that are not covered.

Given the international consensus on the importance of the family to the lives of children with disabilities, it is worth looking at general family support policies in several countries. Table C-3 summarizes family support policies in Australia, Canada, Israel, Japan, Sweden, and the United Kingdom. Among the findings are the following:

• All of the countries provide a basic family allowance;
• Australia and the United Kingdom provide an additional allowance for low-income families;
• Quebec, Israel, and the United Kingdom provide a grant for the birth of a child;
• Quebec and the United Kingdom provide an additional allowance for families with young children;
• Israel, Sweden, and the United Kingdom provide an additional allowance for large families; and
• Sweden and the United Kingdom provide a housing allowance.[22]

Table C-3 suggests once again that supports and services for children with disabilities must be considered in light of overall efforts to support families.

Table C-3 GENERAL FAMILY SUPPORT PROGRAMS, SELECTED COUNTRIES

Country	Australia	Canada	Canada (Quebec)	Israel	Japan	Sweden	United Kingdom
Basic Family Allowance	yes	yes	yes	yes	yes	yes	yes
Low Income Supplement	yes						yes
Birth Grant			yes	yes			yes
Young Child Supplement			yes				yes
Large Family Supplement				yes		yes	yes
Housing Allowance						yes	yes

Source: International Social Security Association, 1992. *The Financing of Benefits Intended for the Family and Their Adjustment to the Cost of Living: Conditions for Entitlement to Family Allowances.*

Notes

17. This appendix was authored by Gordon Mermin of the Urban Institute.

18. Alan Gartner, Dorothy Kerzner Lipsky, and Ann P. Turnbull. *Supporting Families with a Child with a Disability: An International Outlook,* Baltimore: Paul H. Brookes Publishing Co., 1991, p. viii.

19. The United Nations Disability Statistics Microcomputer Data Base, Version 1 contains disability statistics from national households surveys, population censuses, and population or civil registration systems of 55 countries. It is the first international data base of its kind (United Nations. *Disability Statistics Compendium,* New York: Publishing Division, United Nations, 1990, p. iii).

20. Scott Campbell Brown, "Towards a Worldwide Surveillance System for Children with Disabilities: Implications for Classification," in *Report from the Task Force on Issues Related to Children for the Revision of the International Classification of Impairments, Disabilities, and Handicaps, August 29–31, 1994, Atlanta, Georgia,* WHO, Document No. SES/ICIDH/C/94.12, Geneva, Switzerland, November 1994.

21. In Canada, only certain provinces provide a child disability allowance.

22. Ilene R. Zeitzer, "Social Insurance Provisions for Children with Disabilities in Selected Industrialized Countries," *Social Security Bulletin* 58 (3, Fall), 1995.

ADDITIONAL INFORMATION NEEDS

Setting priorities is made much more difficult by the lack of information on many of the service needs and program uses of children with disabilities and their families. Even basic data and information on the children benefiting from many programs are not available anywhere today. Better information can help inform and guide the choices that need to be made in improving the system of government programs serving children with disabilities. Some of the most promising avenues we have discovered in the course of this study follow.

Measuring Needs

- A basic question on which there is minimal research is what (if any) are the **total additional service needs and costs associated with raising a child with a disability?**[23] Under what conditions and types of disabilities do these needs and costs arise? There are many related questions, only some of which are noted here. What are the limitations on measuring and valuing different types of needs? How do costs vary according to the type and severity of disability, and characteristics of the child, family, and community? What are the opportunity costs, particularly in lost earnings, associated with caring for a child with different types of disability? What are the marginal costs associated with having more than one child with a disability in a single family?
- In addition to assessing the needs and costs incurred by families, we require a better understanding of **the extent to which different types of programs address those needs and at what costs.** This requires research into the relationship between household budgets and assistance levels. How are cash benefits currently spent? For example, to what extent do educational programs or Medicaid fail to provide the most appropriate services? What are the costs in terms of forgone opportunities or enforcement efforts of alternative

mechanisms, such as vouchers, for providing educational, medical, and other assistance?
• There is a significant dearth of **longitudinal or time series data tracking individuals** receiving program services and measuring the extent to which these services enhance the well-being of children and families or reduce the impact of physical or mental limitations over time. While some data do exist, such as the National Longitudinal Transition Study of Special Education Students, large national longitudinal surveys such as the Survey of Income and Program Participation could collect information about service and program participation of children with disabilities. Currently, the SIPP does not even gather information on SSI participation of young children. Ideally, data should allow one to examine the complex interrelationships among needs, individual and family characteristics, program services, and outcomes. Important questions that might be explored are what different service combinations produce the most efficient and effective outcomes? What types of outcomes (e.g., educational outcomes, work outcomes) are most responsive to various interventions? What are the broader impacts of program participation on all families and different types of families? Or, to reverse the order, in which jurisdictions do individual circumstances improve most on average?

Benefit Use and Program Participation

• There is a critical demand for a **much more complete accounting of the types and values of benefits delivered through programs** for children with disabilities. Ideally, federal, state, and local programs would produce statements of benefits received by each beneficiary, and these administrative data would be merged and analyzed regularly. As long as existing accounting systems are poor and uncoordinated, if they exist at all, it is difficult to determine appropriate benefit levels for a program, or whether existing allocations are appropriate. Even where valuation of benefits is difficult, the statistical system should determine which children participate in more than one program, whether there is duplication of services, and, when identifiable, the extent to which needs are not being addressed, perhaps because of waiting lists.
• **Comprehensive and well-designed audit data can be a valuable source of information for non-audit purposes.** Audits or extensive reviews of specific cases within programs can be used to improve programs. Audit information can provide statistics on the preva-

lence of actual or possible errors in eligibility determination or benefit provision, whether due to individual uncertainty, fraud, or confusion caused by government rules and information systems. Audit data can also be used to explore other avenues for improving both policymaking and administration. For example, audit information can provide clues to where complex disability eligibility criteria are most difficult to implement and could be revised. An analogy might be drawn with the Taxpayer Compliance Measurement Program (TCMP) that IRS applies to taxpayers. This type of program, although at times controversial, subjects a small sample of taxpayers to a rather intense review, with the sample drawn so as to yield estimates of problems for the population as a whole. Even less comprehensive audits, however, can be used to draw out population-wide estimates of the size of particular problems.

Incentives

- Although we were able to delineate some of the **incentives and disincentives created by the structure of current programs**, we could provide only mild conjecture as to the extent to which these structures change the behavior of beneficiaries, administrators, or policymakers. We believe that more research into these incentive structures is required if their full impact on programs—and related items such as costs, arbitrariness of benefit determination, and potential for inhibiting individual development—is to be better understood.

We recognize that it is common for analyses to end with recommendations for yet more study. In the case of programs for children with disabilities, however, decision-making is especially hampered by lack of data—in particular, on the relationship between disability and the use and demand for public and private resources. We are confirmed in that view by the requirement that led us in the first place to pull together in one place estimates of the size, extent, cost, and participation levels of current programs. Another telling signal is the lack of integrated administrative data through which existing programs can be described and analyzed. The potential gain from such efforts is significant: they include an enhanced ability to direct resources more closely to needs, treat individuals more fairly and equitably, operate programs more effectively, and further develop the individual abilities of the children who are served.

Note

23. While we recognize that the answer to this question depends on the exact nature of the disability, family and community characteristics, etc., no estimates for families with specific characteristics are available.

ABOUT THE AUTHORS

Laudan Y. Aron joined the Urban Institute's Human Resources Policy Center as a research associate in 1992. Her research interests span a wide range of social welfare issues and include child welfare and child support, health, disability, and family planning, education, employment and training, and homelessness. She is currently studying how child welfare agencies deal with domestic violence issues.

Pamela J. Loprest is an economist in the Urban Institute's Income and Benefits Policy Center. Her research focuses on labor market, health insurance, and disability policy issues. She is the author of studies on the connection between disability and work, gender differences in disability, AFDC participation and disability, and health insurance coverage of elderly persons with disabilities.

Eugene Steuerle is a senior fellow at the Urban Institute and author of a column, "Economic Perspective," for *Tax Notes* magazine. He has worked under four different presidents on a wide variety of social, budget, and tax reforms, including service as Deputy Assistant Secretary of the Treasury for Tax Analysis and as Economic Coordinator of the Treasury's 1984–86 tax reform effort. He is the author or co-author of over 150 books, articles, reports, and testimonies, including the recent Urban Institute Press books *Retooling Social Security for the 21st Century* and *The Tax Decade*.